Deep Learning Frameworks for Driver Drowsiness Prediction

Affan Kinu

TABLE OF CONTENTS

LIST OF FIGURES

LIST OF TABLES

LIST OF TABLES

LIST OF ABBREVIATIONS

Abbreviations	Full Forms
ADAS	Advanced Driver Assistance Systems
AFW	Annotated Faces in-the-Wild
AI	Artificial intelligence
AUC	Area under the curve
CNOT	Controlled-NOT
ConNN	Convolutional Neural Network
DL	Deep learning
EAR	Eye aspect ratio
ECG	Electrocardiography
EDA	Electrodermal activity
EEG	Electroencephalography
EMG	Electromyography
FAR	Facial Aspect Ratio
FCNN	Fully connected neural network
FSA	Flamingo Search Algorithm
GANs	Generative Adversarial Networks
GCNs	Graph convolutional networks
GSR	Galvanic skin response
HQCNN	Quantum-classical neural network
ITS	Intelligent transportation systems
KNN	K-Nearest Neighbours

KSS	Karolinska Sleepiness Scale
LFPW	Labeled Face Parts in-the-Wild
LGBM	Light Gradient-Boosting Machine
LoV	Loss of Vigilance
MAR	Mouth aspect ratio
MCNN	Multi-Scale Convolutional Neural Network
ML	Machine learning
MoRTH	Ministry of Road Transport and Highways
MSCNN	Multi-scale CNN
MSE	Mean Squared Error
NAS	Neural architecture search
NISQ	Noisy Intermediate-Scale Quantum
PnP	Perspective-n-Point
PPG	Photoplethysmography
PQC	Parameterized quantum circuit
QCNNs	quantum-classical convolutional neural networks
QML	Quantum machine learning
QML	Quantum-inspired machine learning
SC	Conductance signals
SEL	Strongly Entangling Layer
SPBO	Student Psychology-Based Optimization
SSS	Stanford Sleepiness Scale
SVM	Support vector machines
TLBO	Teaching-Learning-Based Optimization

LIST OF NOTATIONS

Symbol	Description
I	Image
LoV	Lack-of-Vigilance
RotY	Rotation gates
$\hat{L}$	landmark position
N	Number
r	Rotation vector
t	Translation vector
$L_{classical}$	Standard cross entropy loss function
$L_{quantum}$	Quantum output loss function

CHAPTER-1

INTRODUCTION

This chapter presents an overview of the context of the research around the thesis. It starts by giving an overall overview of the research background, problem, and research driving forces. It then briefly mentions the primary contributions, research objectives, and the overall thesis outline.

1.1 BACKGROUND

Transportation is a fundamental element of human civilization, as it helps move people, goods, and services over long distances, brings together communities, boosts the economy, and improves day-to-day life (Rodrigue et al., 2020). Among the various modes of transport, road transport is the most prominent due to its versatility, ease of use, and door-to-door coverage. As the use of motor vehicles has spread to private, commercial, and public means, road transportation has evolved into a pillar of contemporary society. Yet, the sharp increase in the number of cars, along with the growth of urban centers, has brought about a troubling rise in road accidents worldwide (Schoeman et al., 2018).

Recent statistics have shown that more than 1.2 million individuals lose their lives each year in road accidents, and almost 50 million are injured, many of which result in lifelong disabilities (World Health Organization, 2023). On the current trend, road traffic injuries are estimated to become the third leading cause of death globally by the year 2025. Not only do they produce human morbidity, but they also impose a significant economic burden on families as well as on national healthcare systems. Figure 1.1 illustrates the road accident data in India according to publicly available information from the Ministry of Road Transport and Highways (MoRTH), Government of India. There are numerous reasons for road accidents, but human faults and driver negligence remain the most dominant. The contributing factors include drunken driving, speeding, distracted driving, poor road conditions, absence of road signs, and unfavorable weather conditions such as fog or rain. Among these factors, a lesser known yet highly dangerous cause is the loss of vigilance resulting from driver drowsiness, fatigue, or sleep deprivation (National Sleep Foundation,

2020). Empirical evidence further highlights the impact of sleep loss on road safety, for instance, Walker, M. (2017), in his book Why We Sleep, reports a measurable increase in traffic accidents during the days when clocks shift forward for daylight saving time, corresponding to the loss of one hour of sleep, thereby reinforcing the critical link between sleep deprivation and accident risk.

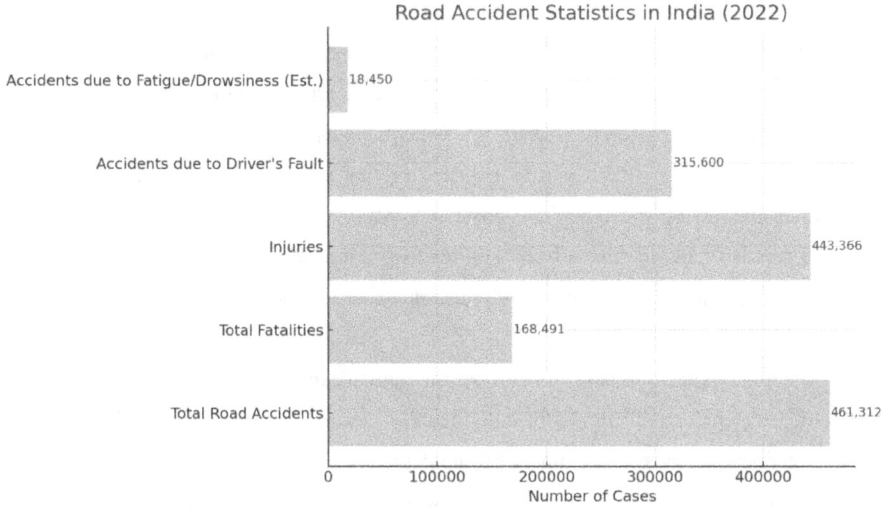

Figure 1. 1. Road accidents in India, 2022 (MoRTH, 2022)

1.1.1 Loss of Vigilance (LoV)

Loss of Vigilance (LoV), also commonly expressed as driver inattention or drowsiness, has become one of the most significant and overlooked causes of road accidents (Ngxande et al., 2017). LoV refers to a gradual reduction in a driver's alertness, usually caused by fatigue, lack of sleep, repetitive driving conditions, or underlying medical conditions. In this altered biological state, a driver's cognitive and motor functions are impaired, making it progressively harder to perceive danger, respond in a timely manner, or maintain correct control of the vehicle (Sahayadhas et al., 2012). Whereas more apparent impairments such as alcohol consumption or mobile phone use are easily detected, drowsiness can develop quietly, often without the driver or others noticing until it is too late.

Drivers may experience microsleeps, which are short and involuntary periods of sleep, or brief lapses in attention lasting only a few seconds, yet these are sufficient to cause severe accidents, particularly at high speeds. The risk associated with LoV is considerably higher during long-duration trips, nighttime driving, or early afternoon hours due to the influence of natural circadian rhythms (Horne et al., 1999). This relationship between sleep deprivation and accident likelihood is further supported by population-level observations reported by Dr. Matthew Walker, who highlights a consistent rise in traffic accidents following daylight saving time transitions, emphasizing the sensitivity of driving performance to even minor sleep loss. Even with the incorporation of modern vehicle safety features such as lane-departure warning systems, adaptive cruise control, and driver assistance technologies, which aim to enhance driving safety, these systems are not fully effective in addressing the biological onset of drowsiness. As a result, LoV continues to remain a pervasive and imminent hazard on roadways, indicating a clear need for smart, non-intrusive surveillance systems capable of real-time detection and timely intervention.

Sleepiness or drowsiness can hamper the human capacity to carry out daily activities. It becomes even more challenging for individuals who perform critical tasks such as driving a vehicle or operating heavy machinery. Sleepiness is defined as an intermediate biological state in which a human being is neither fully awake nor fully asleep (Nojiri et al., 2019). One of the earliest manifestations of sleepiness is difficulty in maintaining the eyes open, which may gradually reduce the individual's ability to perform even simple tasks. As the condition progresses, the person may begin to doze off, accompanied by involuntary head or body movements, such as forward or backward swaying. Repetitive yawning is another commonly observed symptom, indicating a high likelihood of sleepiness. When such symptoms appear, the individual is generally not fit to engage in attention-demanding activities like driving (Chai et al., 2019).

Individuals typically do not fall asleep suddenly or involuntarily; rather, drowsiness develops progressively due to multiple contributing factors. These factors include lack of sufficient sleep or the presence of sleep disorders, certain health conditions, the effects of medication or drugs, and poor lifestyle habits. Sleep disorders constitute one of the major causes of drowsiness and are often associated with other medical complications. Even when individuals are aware of their sleep-related conditions, they may still choose to drive, and it remains difficult to discourage such behavior (Lagarde and Batejat, 1994). Medical conditions such as thyroid imbalance, abnormal blood glucose levels, liver impairment, or obesity can also contribute to fatigue and drowsiness. Similarly, medications including antidepressants, insulin, or antihistamines may impair alertness, with effects varying across individuals (Sunwoo et al., 2017). Unfortunately, such individuals often tend to undercompensate for risk and continue driving despite reduced vigilance.

Several studies further indicate that a sedentary lifestyle can predispose individuals to sleep disorders and daytime drowsiness (Yang et al., 2017; Hemant Kumar et al., 2017). It is important to differentiate between fatigue and drowsiness, as fatigue typically results from physical exertion or illness, whereas drowsiness represents the transitional state preceding sleep. From a road safety perspective, drowsiness poses a greater threat than fatigue. Driving is a complex task that demands sustained attention and coordinated physical and mental responses, and a sleepy driver is particularly dangerous because sleepiness is a well-established risk factor for road traffic accidents (Meshram et al., 2015). Such drivers often exhibit reduced focus on the road, slower reaction times in emergency situations, and poor or delayed decision-making. Additional contributing factors to driver drowsiness include alcohol consumption, even within legal limits, obesity, depression, shift work, extended periods of driving without adequate rest, and nighttime driving. Self-confidence in one's perceived wakefulness can also act as a contributing factor, as drivers may overestimate their alertness and underestimate the associated risks (Abulkhair et al., 2015).

1.2 RESEARCH MOTIVATION

Transportation is the pillar of contemporary civilization that facilitates the movement of goods and people from city to city, region to region, and country to country. Among all forms, road transport is the most common mode, as it links distant locations and supports business logistics through buses, trucks, cars, and motorbikes. Its cost-effectiveness, door-to-door reachability, and operational flexibility render it indispensable in both urban and rural environments. However, despite these advantages, road transport continues to face serious safety challenges, particularly the increasing number of vehicle collisions worldwide. One of the primary causes of such collisions is the lack of vigilance (LoV) among drivers, which commonly arises due to fatigue, inattention, and drowsiness.

A significant number of traffic crashes occurring globally each year are attributed to drowsy driving, resulting in loss of life, severe injuries, and substantial economic costs to individuals and governments. Prolonged driving hours and sleep deprivation further aggravate the risk of LoV, where even short lapses in attention can lead to catastrophic consequences. Due to this growing concern, researchers and engineers across the world are increasingly focusing on the development of automated driver monitoring systems capable of detecting early signs of fatigue and reduced alertness. However, most existing solutions continue to suffer from limitations such as computational inefficiency, limited resilience to instantaneous behavioral fluctuations, slow response times, and reliance on intrusive sensing mechanisms. These shortcomings highlight the need for smart, fast, and non-intrusive drowsiness detection and alert systems that can operate effectively in real driving environments.

The motivation of the present research is to design a computationally lightweight, fast, scalable, and context-sensitive LoV detection system that can accurately identify the driver's sleep state and recognize it sufficiently early to trigger timely preventive alerts. By utilizing multiple visual and behavioral cues and integrating deep learning, fuzzy logic, and hybrid learning models, this research aims to contribute toward safer road transportation and intelligent driver assistance systems, with a strong emphasis on real-world deployment feasibility across diverse driver profiles and varying environmental conditions.

1.3 OVERVIEW OF THE SUCCINCT LITERATURE REVIEW

Over the past decade, the detection of LoV in drivers, which is commonly manifested as drowsiness, has emerged as an important area of research due to its significant implications for road safety, human health, and intelligent transportation systems. Previous works categorize drowsiness detection techniques into three broad groups, which predominantly fall under biological signal-based techniques, vehicle behavior-based techniques, and image-based techniques (Ramzan et al., 2019), (Mousavikia et al., 2022). Biological-based methods utilize physiological signals such as ElectroEncephaloGraphy (EEG), electrocardiography (ECG), ElectroOculoGram (EOG), and skin conductivity in order to determine drowsiness (Hou et al., 2022), (Pradhan et al., 2023). Although these methods provide clinically reliable indicators, they often rely on intrusive sensor placement, which limits their practicality in real-world driving environments.

On the other hand, vehicle-based approaches analyze driving behavior such as steering angle, lane deviation, or pedal activity to infer the vigilance state of the driver (Jasim and Hassan, 2022), (Sharma et al., 2022). Emerging trends increasingly emphasize non-invasive, image-based solutions that track facial parameters such as eye closure, yawning frequency, and head orientation to estimate drowsiness levels (Elidrissi et al., 2023), (Jasim and Hassan, 2022). Nevertheless, these systems remain hindered by practical challenges including facial occlusions caused by glasses or masks, variations in illumination conditions, and inter-subject facial and behavioral diversity. Despite these limitations, image-based solutions continue to gain preference due to their usability, scalability, and non-intrusive nature.

In recent years, Deep Learning (DL) and Artificial Intelligence (AI) have become powerful tools in this domain, enabling computational models to learn complex patterns from facial images and behavioral cues (Zhao et al., 2020), (Nasri et al., 2023), (Véras et al., 2023). However, a common limitation of many AI-based systems lies in their reliance on single-feature analysis, such as Eye Aspect Ratio (EAR) alone, which restricts system flexibility in real-world scenarios where drivers may exhibit subtle, overlapping, or mixed indicators of drowsiness. Current literature trends further reflect a growing interest in multimodal and hybrid approaches that combine visual and physiological information to improve detection accuracy. Nevertheless, when deployed on resource-limited platforms, such approaches often face significant challenges related to real-time processing constraints. Furthermore, Deep Learning architectures such as Convolutional Neural Networks (CNNs) and Recurrent Neural Networks (RNNs) have demonstrated promising performance in drowsiness detection tasks; however, they typically require substantial computational resources and large volumes of labeled data, which complicates their deployment in embedded and real-time systems. Therefore, despite considerable progress in driver drowsiness detection research, persistent limitations remain with respect to generalization capability, early-stage detection, adaptability to dynamic conditions, and overall computational efficiency.

1.4 RESEARCH GAPS

In spite of the wide-ranging research conducted in the area of driver drowsiness detection, several practical and methodological challenges continue to limit the effectiveness of existing systems. Numerous prior studies have demonstrated promising performance in controlled laboratory or simulation environments; however, they often fail to translate effectively to real-world driving scenarios due to environmental variability and operational constraints (e.g., Ramzan et al., 2019; Mousavikia et al., 2022). A critical analysis of the literature reveals recurring limitations such as poor generalization, limited adaptability, and high computational demand, which collectively make many existing schemes unsuitable for real-time deployment. The major research gaps identified from the literature are discussed below, along with brief indications of how this thesis addresses them.

A significant portion of existing approaches relies predominantly on a single behavioral characteristic, most commonly eye closure measured through Eye Aspect Ratio (EAR). While EAR is a useful indicator, exclusive dependence on a single cue ignores the complementary nature of other behavioral signals such as yawning frequency, blink duration, head tilt, and gaze deviation, which together provide a more reliable representation of driver vigilance. This research addresses this limitation by adopting a multi-feature framework that integrates several facial and behavioral indicators to improve early and accurate detection of drowsiness.

Another major challenge lies in the poor robustness of visual-based models under real-world conditions, including partial facial occlusion caused by glasses or masks, variable illumination, and inter-individual differences in facial structure and behavior. Such factors often lead to inconsistent performance in dynamic driving environments. To mitigate this issue, the proposed work emphasizes contextual feature extraction and adaptive decision-making mechanisms designed to operate reliably under varying visual and environmental conditions.

Many existing systems further rely on binary classification or fixed threshold-based decision strategies, which are inadequate for handling ambiguous or transitional vigilance states commonly observed in real driving scenarios. Human alertness does not change abruptly, and therefore rigid classification models fail to capture gradual loss of vigilance. This research addresses this gap by introducing adaptive decision models that classify drowsiness into multiple levels, thereby emulating more human-like reasoning and enabling timely and context-aware interventions.

Although Deep Learning models such as Convolutional Neural Networks and Recurrent Neural Networks demonstrate strong classification capabilities, their dependency on large datasets and high computational resources limit their suitability for embedded automotive platforms. For example, many in-vehicle systems are equipped with low-power CPUs and limited memory resources, which are insufficient to support computationally intensive deep models in real time. While cloud-based processing may appear as an alternative, it introduces latency, connectivity dependency, and reliability concerns, making it impractical for safety-critical automotive applications. For this reason, the present research explicitly focuses on lightweight model design and efficient feature representation to ensure feasibility on resource-constrained platforms.

Furthermore, existing solutions often emphasize a single type of indicator, either visual or behavioral, without effectively combining multiple complementary cues. Such isolated approaches fail to capture the complex and dynamic nature of driver behavior. In contrast, this thesis adopts a fusion-based strategy that integrates insights from classical machine learning, deep learning, and fuzzy logic to interpret driver behavior more comprehensively in real time, particularly under fluctuating physical and emotional states. Overall, these identified gaps collectively motivate the need for a robust, adaptive, and computationally efficient driver drowsiness detection framework, which forms the core focus of the proposed research.

1.5 RESEARCH QUESTIONS

The complexity of detecting driver drowsiness in real-world scenarios, which are often characterized by uncertain and dynamic behavioral conditions, calls for adaptive and intelligent systems that go beyond conventional threshold-based techniques. The following research questions are formulated to guide the direction of this work and to address the critical challenges identified during the study.

- **RQ1:** Considering challenges such as individual differences, environmental variability, facial occlusion, and partial face obstruction, how can multiple complementary visual features extracted from facial regions be effectively integrated and fused to reliably distinguish between alertness and varying levels of sleepiness?

- **RQ2:** What methods can enhance the extraction, fusion, and interpretation of behavioral signals such as eye movement, mouth movement, and head direction in order to support consistent and real-time detection of driver drowsiness under dynamic driving conditions?
- **RQ3:** What techniques can be employed to design the proposed detection system in a computationally lightweight, fast, and scalable manner, suitable for real-time implementation on resource-limited embedded platforms, without sacrificing accuracy and reliability?
- **RQ4:** How can improving the internal representation and combination of input features contribute to enhanced generalization capability and robustness of the detection system across a wide range of driver profiles, behavioral patterns, and driving environments?

1.6 PROPOSED RESEARCH WORK

It has been identified that, even with advancements in artificial intelligence and driver monitoring systems, most of the previous schemes remain limited in their practical applicability due to issues such as slow response times, high computational requirements, limited contextual awareness, and poor adaptability under real-world driving scenarios. Therefore, the proposed research work attempts to address the critical need for a robust, non-invasive, and real-time Loss of Vigilance (LoV) detection solution by combining deep learning, classical machine learning, fuzzy logic, and hybrid quantum–classical neural network approaches to achieve accurate and timely LoV detection.

1.6.1 Title of the thesis

The title of the thesis is stated at this stage to clearly define the thematic focus and scope of the proposed research work:

"Novel Visual Contextual Framework for Reliable Detection of Lack of Vigilance in a Driver"

1.6.2 Aim of the thesis

The prime aim of the proposed research work is to introduce a novel, cost-effective computational framework that extracts visual contextual information in order to accurately identify the LoV state in a driver in real time

1.6.3 Objectives of the Research Work

The specific objectives of the proposed research work are defined as follows:

i). To develop a contextual framework using deep learning techniques to identify patterns associated with LoV states.

ii). To design an integrated machine learning and deep learning system for robust identification of facial landmarks under diverse environmental and operational conditions.

iii). To develop a fuzzy logic-based model that utilizes logged events, iris movement, and head position for improved and adaptive drowsiness detection.

iv). To explore the implementation of hybrid quantum–classical neural networks for enhanced feature extraction and reliable LoV detection.

1.7 ORIGINAL CONTRIBUTION

In the context of this thesis, the term *original contribution* refers to the novel integration, adaptation, and contextual application of multiple computational techniques to address the problem of driver drowsiness (Lack of Vigilance) detection in real-world driving environments. The proposed research introduces a comprehensive, multi-layered framework that goes beyond conventional single-indicator or isolated-feature approaches commonly reported in the literature. Unlike traditional systems that rely on rigid thresholds or binary decision logic, this work presents a context-aware and real-time computational framework capable of adapting to uncertainty, inter-driver variability, and dynamic driving conditions. The originality of the research lies not in the isolated use of individual techniques, but in their systematic integration, real-time feasibility, adaptive decision-making capability, and progressive validation across multiple implementation phases. In addition, an exploratory hybrid quantum–classical learning model is investigated and reported as a forward-looking study to assess the feasibility of emerging computational paradigms for future driver monitoring systems. The original contributions of this research are summarized in Table 1.1.

Table 1. 1. Original contribution of the proposed research work

Framework	Solution Approach	Significance	Applicability
Framework 1 *Analyzing driver alertness using contextual image information*	A deep learning-based image classification model is developed and trained on a custom dataset incorporating variations in facial occlusion, pose, and lighting conditions.	This framework addresses the low reliability of single-frame analysis and is effective in enhancing generalization under practical driving conditions.	Suitable for real-time driver monitoring systems, automotive safety platforms, and transport analytics tools.
Framework 2 *Detecting behavioral cues from facial indicators in live conditions*	A facial landmark regression task is modelled using Support Vector Regression (SVR) to track eye and mouth metrics such as Eye Aspect Ratio (EAR) and Mouth Aspect Ratio (MAR), and is integrated with deep learning models for real-time alert generation.	This framework mitigates inconsistent facial landmark detection under occlusion and motion, while ensuring continuous behaviour tracking with low-latency response.	Deployable in dashboard-based monitoring units, in-cabin camera systems, and mobile driver assistance applications.
Framework 3 *Adaptive fuzzy-based decision system for interpreting behavioral indicators*	A fuzzy logic-based decision framework is implemented using multi-feature inputs including EAR, MAR, blink rate, head pose, and iris movement to classify vigilance levels adaptively.	This framework addresses the rigidity of binary classification models and improves decision reliability under uncertain real-world conditions by enabling human-like adaptive reasoning with reduced false positives.	Applicable to long-haul logistics, public transportation systems, and personalized fatigue-aware driver assistance tools.
Framework 4 (Exploratory)	A hybrid quantum–classical neural network is	This framework aims to improve feature	Forward-compatible with

Hybrid learning scheme for improved feature interpretation	explored by combining Convolutional Neural Network (CNN)-based feature extraction with quantum feature encoding and entanglement layers.	discrimination efficiency and adaptability while reducing computational overhead compared to conventional deep models.	edge-AI platforms and next-generation intelligent vehicle safety systems.

1.8 ORGANIZATION OF THE THESIS

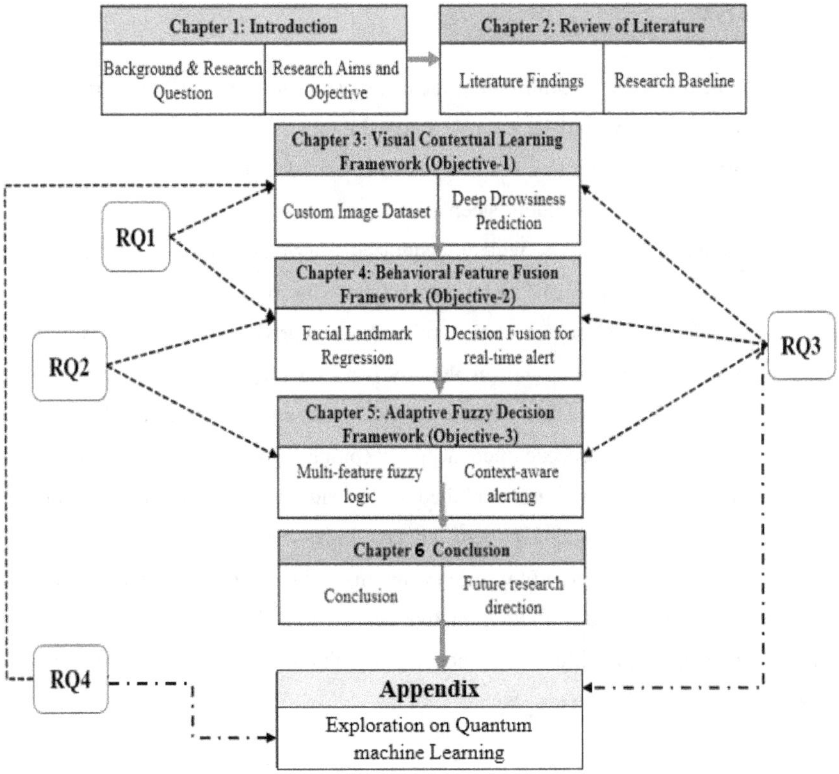

Figure 1. 2. A schematic structure of the Thesis outline

CHAPTER-2

REVIEW OF LITERATURE

This chapter presents a structured review of existing research related to driver attention, fatigue, and drowsiness detection. The primary objective is to analyze recent developments, identify dominant methodological trends, and understand the practical limitations associated with previously proposed approaches. Through this review, key research challenges are identified, which provide the foundation for motivating the proposed multi-stage and context-aware detection framework developed in this thesis.

2.1 OVERVIEW

Driver drowsiness is a major contributing factor to a significant proportion of road accidents worldwide, as it directly impairs cognitive functioning, reduces alertness, slows reaction time, and degrades the ability to make timely and correct decisions that are essential for safe driving. Prolonged driving duration, sleep deprivation, monotonous road environments, and physical or mental exhaustion are widely recognized contributors to the onset of drowsiness, thereby making it a critical and persistent concern for overall road safety. Figure 2.1 illustrates a typical visual representation of a drowsy driver, characterized by drooping eyelids, slumped body posture, and involuntary head nodding, which are among the most commonly reported observable behavioral manifestations in the literature. These indicators are frequently observed to precede microsleeps or complete loss of driver attention, and they serve as fundamental visual cues exploited by a wide range of driver monitoring and drowsiness detection techniques. Also, many image-based and behavioral analysis approaches rely on such externally visible symptoms to infer internal vigilance degradation. Therefore, the figure provides a representative depiction of the physical symptoms that are repeatedly analyzed, quantified, and modeled by the detection methods reviewed and discussed throughout this chapter.

Figure 2.1. A visual example of a driver experiencing drowsiness (Nasri, 2022)

In recent years, researchers have proposed various methods to detect driver drowsiness, which can be broadly classified into two major groups, namely subjective measures and objective measures, as illustrated in Figure 2.2. The objective measures are further categorized into three distinct classes, namely vehicle-based measures, physiological measures, and behavioral measures, depending on the nature of the information source, sensing mechanism, and analysis strategy employed. This hierarchical classification is widely adopted in the literature, as it provides a structured understanding of how different indicators of driver vigilance are captured, processed, and interpreted under diverse driving conditions.

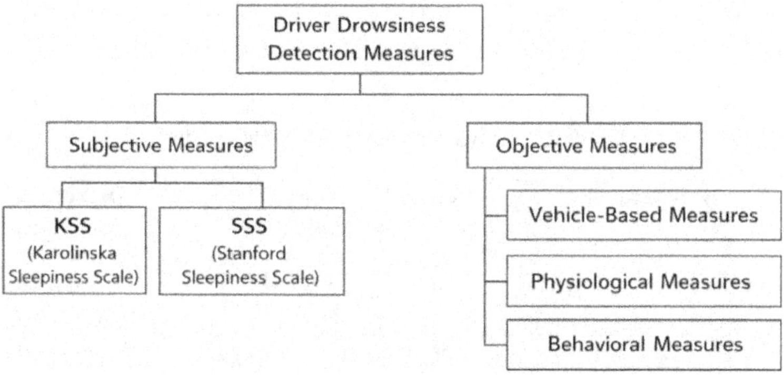

Figure 2.2. Classification of driver drowsiness detection approaches

The subjective measures are primarily based on self-reporting techniques, in which drivers explicitly communicate their perceived level of alertness or sleepiness. These approaches commonly rely on questionnaires, surveys, and standardized sleepiness rating scales such as the Stanford Sleepiness Scale (SSS) (Hoddes et al., 1973) and the Karolinska Sleepiness Scale (KSS) (Åkerstedt and Gillberg, 1994). The KSS is a 9-point Likert scale ranging from "extremely alert" to "very sleepy", where scores between 1 and 4 represent an alert state, values from 5 to 7 indicate increasing levels of drowsiness, and scores of 8 or 9 correspond to near-sleep or sleep onset conditions. Table 2.1 highlights the KSS with different states of driver drowsiness as reported in the literature

Table 2.1. KSS scale with different driver state

KSS Scale	Verbal Description	Driver State
1	Extremely Alert	Awake State
2	Very Alert	Awake State
3	Alert	Awake State
4	Fairly Alert	Awake State
5	Neither Alert nor Sleepy	Drowsy State
6	Initial signs of Sleepiness	Drowsy State
7	Sleepy, no effort to stay alert	Drowsy State
8	Sleepy, effort to stay alert	Sleepy State
9	Very Sleepy, more effort to stay alert	Sleepy State

On the other hand, SSS uses a 7-point scale where levels 1 to 3 describe alertness, levels 4 to 5 suggest drowsiness, and levels 6 to 7 signify deep sleepiness and reduced ability to stay awake. Table 2.2 highlights the SSS with different state of the driver.

Table 2.2. SSS scale with different driver state

SSS Scale	Verbal Description	Driver State
1	Feeling Active, Vital, and Alert	Awake State
2	Able to Concentrate, but not as Active	Awake State
3	Awake, But Not Fully Alert	Awake State
4	Somewhat Foggy, Let Down	Drowsy State
5	Foggy, Losing Interest to Stay Awake	Drowsy State
6	Sleepy, Struggling to Stay Awake	Sleepy State
7	Sleep Onset Soon, Dream-like Thoughts	Sleepy State

The KSS- and SSS-based ratings are often integrated into experimental driving simulators, where drivers verbally or manually indicate their perceived state of alertness using a microphone, touchscreen interface, or structured prompts. However, these subjective methods are primarily effective only within controlled experimental environments and are not suitable for real-world autonomous drowsiness detection systems, as they are subject to multiple inherent limitations, such as self-reporting bias, delayed response, and the tendency of participants to consciously or unconsciously overestimate their level of alertness in safety-critical situations.

As shown in Figure 2.2, the objective measures are divided into three major categories, as they are quantifiable and provide observable data collected through various sensors and analyzed using computational techniques. Unlike subjective approaches, these methods do not rely on self-assessment, and this makes them more reliable and consistent for real-time and automated driver drowsiness detection applications. The different categories of objective measures are briefly discussed as follows.

- **Vehicle-Based Measures:** These approaches monitor variations in vehicle dynamics such as steering angle, steering wheel movement, lane departure frequency, acceleration and braking patterns, speed variability, and overall driving duration. Such parameters are typically acquired through in-vehicle sensors, CAN bus data, or advanced driver assistance systems, and even minor deviations from normal driving patterns can indicate a gradual loss of driver alertness, for example erratic lane keeping, delayed steering correction, or unstable speed control. When these parameters are processed using machine learning algorithms or rule-based models, as reported in several state-of-the-art studies (e.g., Jasim and Hassan, 2022; Sharma et al., 2022), they can provide early signals indicating the onset of drowsiness. In this thesis, vehicle-based indicators are reviewed as part of the literature; however, the proposed framework primarily focuses on visual and behavioral cues rather than direct vehicle telemetry.

- **Physiological Measures:** This category involves the processing of bio-signals such as EEG, ECG, ElectroMyoGraphy (EMG), ElectroDermalActivity (EDA), and PhotoPlethysmoGraphy (PPG). These signals are typically measured through wearable or contact-based sensors and are analyzed using signal processing techniques or deep learning models to differentiate between alert and drowsy states, as demonstrated in prior works (e.g., Hou et al., 2022; Pradhan et al., 2023). The main advantage of physiological measures lies in their high sensitivity to internal state changes of the human body. However, since they require sensors to be attached to the driver's body, practical deployment in everyday driving scenarios can be challenging due to setup complexity and user acceptance considerations.

- **Behavioral Measures:** Behavioral approaches are among the most widely adopted techniques in commercial and research-oriented drowsiness detection systems, primarily due to their non-intrusive nature. These methods focus on visual and motion-based cues such as eye blink rate, eyelid closure duration, yawning frequency, head nodding, facial expressions, and gaze direction. The extracted features are typically processed using advanced models such as Convolutional Neural Networks (CNNs), Recurrent Neural Networks (RNNs), or hybrid CNN–LSTM architectures, as reported in several studies (e.g., Zhao et al., 2020; Véras et al., 2023). Although these methods are practical and scalable, the overall detection accuracy strongly depends on appropriate model selection, data preprocessing strategies, and robustness to lighting variation and facial occlusion.

Although the primary focus of this work is driver drowsiness detection, the literature review presented in this chapter also encompasses closely related aspects such as driver attention and driver fatigue, owing to their strong causal relationship with drowsiness. Since drowsiness often emerges as a progressive outcome of sustained fatigue and reduced attentional capacity, understanding the factors that precede and contribute to its development is essential for designing early-stage detection mechanisms rather than reactive systems. In addition, it is observed that many methods employed in attention and fatigue analysis such as physiological signal processing, vehicle behavior analysis, and image-based feature extraction are mainly shared with drowsiness detection frameworks, thereby justifying their inclusion in this review.

2.2 REVIEW OF THE STUDIES ON MONITORING DRIVER'S ATTENTION

In recent years, some researchers have investigated the use of physiological and in-vehicle sensor technology to monitor drivers' attention levels to identify early warnings of drowsiness or fatigue. These studies used various bio signals such as EEG, ECG, EMG and PPG, as well as other behavioural characteristics such as steering grip force, heart rate variability and eye movements. The research done by (Doudou et al., 2023) did an extensive comparison of the method design of detecting sleep using physiological sensors. They compared different commercially available sensors and compared them with respect to their cost, size, and performance. Their study primarily addresses the issue of selecting efficient hardware suitable for driver monitoring but not addressing how to combine these devices in fully operational systems or how they perform under real driving conditions.

In a more precise line of thought, Satti et al. (2021) developed a system that monitors muscle activity in the driver's forearms using EMG signals captured from microneedle array electrodes embedded in the steering wheel. The signals were recorded during a controlled one-hour simulated driving session, and the reduction in muscle activation patterns was used as an indicator of driver drowsiness. Although the proposed system demonstrated promising performance due to the use of novel electrode design, the analysis was restricted to a single muscular signal and did not incorporate complementary visual or behavioural cues such as eye closure, head movement, or facial dynamics. This limitation reduces its effectiveness in capturing the multifactorial nature of driver drowsiness in real-world driving scenarios.

The study conducted by Murugan et al. (2023) extended bio signal-based drowsiness detection by incorporating multiple physiological signals, including EEG, ECG, EOG, and EMG. However, their final classification framework primarily relied on features extracted from EOG signals, which were subsequently classified using a swarm intelligence–based machine learning model. The proposed method achieved high performance in a binary classification setting (drowsy vs. alert); however, its accuracy degraded when additional drowsiness levels were introduced, such as multi-stage fatigue classification aligned with subjective sleepiness scales (e.g., Karolinska Sleepiness Scale). Furthermore, the dataset used in the study was relatively small and collected under controlled conditions, which constrains the generalization capability of the model when deployed in diverse real-world driving environments. Similarly, Ren et al. (2021) proposed a specialized neural network architecture for fatigue detection using EEG signals, focusing on discriminative patterns in brain wave activity. The reported results indicate an accuracy exceeding 92% under laboratory conditions. Nevertheless, the experimental setup involved a limited number of participants and lacked exposure to challenging real-life driving conditions such as variable illumination, head pose changes, and prolonged driving durations. Consequently, the scalability and practical applicability of the proposed EEG-based approach in real-world driver monitoring systems remain uncertain.

Other researchers looked at cardiac signals. For example, Lee et al. (2019) investigated heart rate variability using both ECG and PhotoPlethysmoGram (PPG) sensors. Instead of directly using raw time-domain signals, the authors transformed the cardiac signals into recurrence plots (RP), which visually encode the temporal dynamics and periodicity of heart rate variations. These recurrence plots were further normalized using a Rectified Linear Unit (ReLU)-based scaling function to enhance discriminative patterns, and the resulting representations were used as inputs to a CNN. The study outcome shows robustness of the model across different sensor types and effective heart rate characterization. However, the experimental analysis was conducted only in a simulated or controlled environment and did not address practical challenges such as motion artifacts, sensor displacement, or body movement effects, which are commonly encountered during real-world driving.

Similarly, Gao et al. (2023) employed EEG signals using a fundamentally different representation strategy. Rather than relying on handcrafted time-domain features, the EEG signals were transformed into time–frequency representations in the form of spectrograms, enabling preservation of both spectral and temporal fatigue-related patterns. These spectrograms were then processed using a hybrid deep learning architecture that integrates CNNs for spatial feature extraction with RNNs to model temporal dependencies across successive EEG segments. Although this approach demonstrates improved performance compared to conventional EEG-based methods, the evaluation relied on publicly available datasets collected under controlled conditions and was not validated in live traffic environments, which may limit its applicability for real-world driver monitoring systems.

Wang et al. (2018) investigated the combination of ECG and EEG signals to assess driver fatigue across different driving phases. They employed palm-based ECG acquisition, which was described as easy to use and non-intrusive, and combined this with EEG recordings to capture both cardiac and neural fatigue indicators. Their evaluation also incorporated subjective self-reports provided by drivers, enabling cross-validation between physiological measurements and perceived fatigue levels. However, a major limitation of this study is that it did not adequately analyse the influence of motion artifacts, steering-induced muscle activity, or external electromagnetic noise on signal quality, which raises concerns regarding robustness under real-world driving conditions. Similarly, Min et al. (2017) focused on EEG-based fatigue detection and enhanced performance by extracting multiple entropy-based features, including sample entropy, spectral entropy, and fuzzy entropy, which are designed to quantify signal complexity and irregularity associated with mental fatigue. The extracted features were evaluated using several machine learning classifiers, namely SVM, k-nearest neighbors (k-NN), and linear discriminant analysis (LDA), achieving high classification accuracy. Furthermore, their channel selection strategy was based on identifying EEG channels that exhibited the highest entropy variation between alert and fatigued states, thereby reducing redundant channels and computational complexity. Despite these strengths, the study involved only twelve participants and was conducted in a simulated driving environment, which limits the generalizability of the results to larger, more diverse driver populations and real-world scenarios.

The work of (Sun et al., 2011) investigated a non-contact method to measure fatigue by identifying heart rate, breathing, and blinking through special sensors located in the vehicle cabin. The system is able to operate over short distances and without the need for physical contact with the driver. It was tested in a simulator and showed good potential for continuous monitoring, but the system's performance on real roads and during longer drives was not evaluated. The above discussed literatures highlight how various biological and sensor-based methods have been explored to monitor driver attention and detect signs of fatigue. As Table 2.3 shows, each method has its strengths, but future studies need to focus more on real-time applications, better generalization, and combining multiple indicators for improved accuracy.

Table 2.3. Highlights of the above discussed literature on monitoring driver's attention

Authors	Problem	Solution	Outcome	Limitation
(Doudou et al., 2023)	Physiological signals; need for low-cost sensors	Reviewed and ranked existing biosensors	Aided hardware selection for detection systems	Focused on hardware; lacked real-world and software analysis
(Satti et al., 2021)	EMG; muscle fatigue from steering grip	EMG-based detection using microneedle electrodes	Accurate real-time detection	Narrow signal scope; limited testing across drivers
(Murugan et al., 2023)	EOG, EEG, ECG, sEMG; hypovigilance detection	ML classifiers with PCA and feature extraction from EOG	98.7% accuracy in binary class; strong ensemble model	Limited dataset; accuracy dropped in multi-class detection
(Ren et al., 2021)	EEG; noisy signal feature extraction	RBF-TLLH neural network with optimized parameters	92.7% accuracy; better than standard ANN models	Small sample; tested only in simulated environment
(Lee et al., 2019)	HRV via ECG/PPG; motion noise in wearables	CNN using recurrence plots (ReLU-RP best)	6–17% higher accuracy across sensor types	Virtual testing only; motion artifacts not deeply addressed
(Gao et al., 2023)	EEG; facial methods unreliable	CRNN with log-Mel spectrogram features	High accuracy and stability vs. 4 existing methods	No real-world testing; relied on public datasets

2.3. REVIEW OF THE STUDIES ON ADDRESSING DRIVER'S FATIGUENESS

Understanding and accurately detecting driver fatigue is a critical requirement for effective driver drowsiness detection, given its well-established relationship with road traffic accidents. Many studies have therefore explored image-based, physiological, and hybrid approaches to identify early signs of fatigue and issue timely warnings to drivers. The work carried out by Anber et al. (2022) proposed two deep learning–based models inspired by the AlexNet architecture (Krizhevsky et al., 2012) to assess driver fatigue using facial cues such as head pose variation and mouth movement patterns. One model employed a transfer learning strategy using a pre-trained AlexNet, whereas the second model integrated features extracted using a SVM classifier prior to deep model training. The authors adopted the SVM-based feature extraction approach to enhance class separability and reduce feature redundancy before classification, particularly aiming to stabilize learning under variations in facial appearance and expression. Based on the experimental evaluation, the SVM-assisted model demonstrated superior performance, achieving an accuracy of 99.65% on the NTHU Driver Drowsiness Detection (NTHU-DDD) dataset (Chen et al., 2016). As the transfer learning–based model did not provide a significant comparative advantage, the study primarily highlights the effectiveness of the SVM-integrated architecture for fatigue recognition.

To address the limitations associated with relying on a single data modality, Karuppusamy and Kang (2020) proposed a multimodal driver fatigue detection system that integrates EEG signals, gyroscope data obtained from wearable inertial sensors, and facial image analysis captured using an in-vehicle camera focused on the driver's face. The proposed multimodal framework achieved an accuracy of 93.91%, demonstrating the advantage of fusing physiological signals, motion dynamics, and visual facial cues for more reliable fatigue assessment. Despite the promising performance, the system was evaluated only in controlled experimental settings and was not validated under real-world driving conditions, limiting its immediate practical applicability. The interaction between driver fatigue and vehicle automation was examined by Arefnezhad et al. (2022), who analysed driver responses across different age groups when operating partially automated driving systems. Their findings indicate that mental workload reduction under automation is more pronounced in older drivers, particularly when fatigue is present, suggesting that age influences how automation mitigates fatigue effects. However, the study relied exclusively on PERCLOS (Percentage of Eye Closure over Time) measurements (Dinges et al., 1998), a visual indicator that quantifies the proportion of time a driver's eyes remain closed beyond a defined threshold. The absence of complementary physiological signals and the lack of real-road experimentation restrict the generalizability of the reported findings.

Camera-based methods have also been explored, as can be seen in the work of (Dziuda *et al.*, 2021), where the authors employed eye-related measures such as PERCLOS, eye closure duration, and eye closure frequency to quantify driver fatigue. Professional truck drivers were evaluated in a controlled simulator environment, and the findings indicated that both PERCLOS and eye closure duration exhibited a strong correlation with drivers' self-rated fatigue levels. While these visual indicators were shown to be effective for fatigue estimation, the study was conducted on a relatively limited sample size and was restricted to simulator-based experiments, with no validation performed under real-world driving conditions. Shang *et al.* (2022) extended the scope of visual fatigue analysis by integrating fatigue detection with emotional state recognition using facial image analysis. The authors employed a lightweight CNN-based architecture to extract visual features and combined fatigue-related indicators such as PERCLOS and yawning with facial emotion recognition to compute a composite driver state score. Although the proposed framework achieved reliable fatigue detection performance, the reported emotion recognition accuracy was limited to 73.32%, which may restrict the robustness of the combined fatigue–emotion inference in complex driving scenarios. Furthermore, the model was not evaluated under diverse real-world operating conditions such as nighttime driving, varying illumination levels, or natural traffic environments, which limits its generalizability for real-time deployment.

In a related domain, Chen *et al.* (2022) developed a backpropagation (BP) neural network framework to model the progressive accumulation of driver fatigue over time, rather than treating fatigue as an instantaneous event. The authors extracted fatigue-related behavioural features such as sustained eye closure and yawning frequency and employed a Sigmoid activation function to smooth temporal variations in the network output, thereby reducing abrupt decision transitions. The proposed temporal modelling strategy improved detection accuracy by up to 8.4% and significantly reduced false alarm rates when compared to a conventional BP neural network. Nevertheless, the system was evaluated exclusively on pre-recorded video sequences, and no real-time or on-road validation was conducted, which limits its applicability for live driver monitoring systems.

Fatigue detection under more complex visual conditions was further investigated by Xiao *et al.* (2022), who designed a system based on a multi-scale facial landmark detection framework. Their approach utilized 23 carefully selected facial landmarks to extract discriminative geometric features, along with threshold-based decision logic to handle variations in facial structure across individuals. The experimental results demonstrated an accuracy exceeding 99% on the HNUFDD (Hunan University Fatigue Driving Dataset), which is a publicly available benchmark dataset designed for driver fatigue analysis. The model was explicitly engineered to operate under challenging scenarios such as side-view facial orientations and grayscale imagery, thereby improving robustness against pose and color variations. However, the performance of the proposed system was not evaluated under adverse environmental conditions such as poor illumination, nighttime driving, or weather-induced visual degradation, leaving its reliability under real-world operating conditions insufficiently validated.

Chen et al., (2020) put a focus on physiological signals and monitored heart rate and breathing through the use of smart bracelets and Doppler radar. Fatigue conditions were identified with differential evolution extreme learning machine and was found to be more accurate compared to previous models such as SVM. The results are encouraging with the understanding that it is dependent on specialized hardware, and the system is only being tested up until now within a lab environment. (Dong et al., 2022) attempted to use visual information to address the distraction and fatigue issues. The presented framework utilizes facial attributes to detect signals such as head movement and yawning and utilizes CNN and random forest classifiers. The outcome shows that this method is computationally efficient and works well on embedded hardware. The study, however, did not examine the effect of lighting, occlusion, or camera position on detection.

A deeper video-based approach was introduced by (Xiang et al., 2022), who used a 3D-CNN with an attention mechanism to analyze video frames and extract temporal features. They also addressed the problem of frame loss using a frame aggregation method. The study outcome claimed that this model achieved 95% accuracy. The work of (Ye et al., 2021) took a slightly different path by combining deep learning with 3D head pose estimation. Their system used the RCAN model, and a head pose estimation algorithm to identify drowsiness using PERCLOS and mouth opening degree. The method performed consistently well across multiple datasets, achieving high eye and mouth detection accuracy. Yet, the system's processing time and real-time responsiveness in a moving vehicle were not clearly addressed.

Some researchers have also introduced some advanced models aimed at improving the reliability and speed of driver fatigue detection. The work of (Zhu et al., 2022) suggested a real-time system that uses facial video sequences to compute features such as EAR, MAR, and PERCLOS through a deep CNN model which is designed to be lightweight and fast. The study outcome showed accurate results without the need for any wearable sensors. However, it only focuses on facial data and does not explore the integration with physiological signals. Considering the idea of analyzing driver behavior over time, (Ed-Doughmi et al., 2020) Detect drowsiness by observing motion patterns in video sequences using a 3D convolutional RNN model. Their model achieved 92% accuracy and showed good potential for immediate use. But because the model was trained on a specific dataset, its reliability under broader real-world conditions remains uncertain.

Some studies have focused on understanding the behavioural effects of driver fatigue without proposing explicit detection frameworks. For instance, He et al. (2023) conducted long-term driving experiments to analyse how passive fatigue influences driver behaviour over extended durations. Their study examined indicators such as pupil diameter variations and steering control patterns, concluding that fatigue severity increases proportionally with driving time. While the findings provide valuable behavioural insights, the study did not introduce any real-time fatigue detection mechanism, limiting its applicability to practical systems. In another study, Kassem et al. (2021) proposed a low-cost fatigue monitoring approach using infrared (IR) sensors to track facial expressions under varying illumination conditions. Their system, referred to as DFLP (Dynamic Facial Landmark Processing), achieved an accuracy of 93.3% and demonstrated reliable performance in both daytime and nighttime environments. Although the approach is lightweight and non-invasive, it did not integrate physiological indicators nor evaluate long-term driver behaviour, which are critical for comprehensive fatigue assessment.

Similarly, Salvati et al. (2021) explored fatigue detection through Heart Rate Variability (HRV) analysis and compared its effectiveness with PERCLOS (Percentage of Eye Closure). The results indicated that HRV, which measures fluctuations in the time intervals between consecutive heartbeats, has strong potential as a non-contact fatigue indicator. However, the study was conducted on a very limited sample size, raising concerns regarding the generalizability of the results to larger populations and more complex real-world driving scenarios.

In the domain of brain signal–based fatigue analysis, Sheykhivand et al. (2022) employed a CNN–LSTM architecture directly on raw EEG signals to identify fatigue patterns across six distinct brain regions. By learning spatial–temporal representations automatically, the model achieved high classification accuracy without requiring manual feature extraction. Despite its strong performance, the approach depends on EEG acquisition hardware, which significantly limits its practicality for deployment in everyday driving environments.

Similarly, Wang et al. (2021) investigated a fatigue mitigation strategy using EEG signals processed through Variational Mode Decomposition (VMD) and entropy-based features, combined with auditory stimulation to enhance driver alertness. Their experimental results demonstrated that non-intrusive auditory cues can temporarily reduce drowsiness during driving tasks. However, the study was conducted entirely under controlled laboratory conditions and did not examine long-term consequences, such as habituation to auditory stimuli, sustained effectiveness over prolonged driving sessions, cognitive fatigue rebound effects, or potential distraction-induced risks during real-world driving.

Zheng et al. (2023) proposed a facial fatigue detection approach combining the MAX–MIN algorithm with the ShuffleNet model. The method estimates adaptive upper and lower thresholds of the eye-to-mouth ratio, achieving high precision and accuracy even under real driving conditions and across different facial structures. However, the approach relies solely on visual information and does not integrate other fatigue-related indicators. On the other hand, He et al. (2024) introduced a non-visual fatigue assessment framework using wristband sensor data, vehicle dynamics, and trip logs, processed through a Bi-LSTM model. The system demonstrated high accuracy in real-world trucking environments, particularly when analysing PPG signals. However, its validation is limited to truck drivers, whose fatigue patterns differ from car drivers due to longer continuous driving durations, monotonous routes, and higher physical workload, raising concerns about generalization to other driver groups.

Additionally, Hu et al. (2024) proposed an EEG-based model termed STFN-BRPS, which combines multi-scale convolution and spatial graph modelling to capture fatigue-related brain signal patterns. Although the model outperformed several existing EEG-based methods and was evaluated in real driving scenarios, the dependence on EEG devices still limits its practicality for everyday use. Li et al., (2024) presented FD-LiteNet, a lightweight CNN model optimized to be created using Neural Architecture Search (NAS) for detecting driver fatigue based on EEG signals. The presented model has been optimized to be run on resource-limited devices such as those placed on vehicles without compromising high accuracy and low computational cost. It also has low retraining costs to adapt with new data. Yet practical problems are untouched since there have been no in-real-life experiments under noisy or driving-in-motion environments. (Peng et al., 2024) studied a multi-source fatigue detection method integrating physiological signals and facial video input. It applies deep learning to learn important metrics automatically without the need for feature selection. It achieves greater than 93% accuracy within a three-second detection time interval, allowing early warning.

Tang et al. (2024) enhanced EEG-based fatigue detection by proposing an attention-guided multi-scale CNN model (MSCNN-CAM) that emphasizes salient EEG features relevant to vigilance estimation. The model achieved extremely high performance on the SEED-VIG (SJTU Emotion EEG Dataset for Vigilance Estimation) dataset. Although the approach outperforms existing state-of-the-art methods, challenges related to real-time EEG acquisition and generalization across different driver populations remain unresolvedAnother efficient and low-cost solution was proposed by Lin et al. (2025) using electrocardiogram (ECG)–based heart rate variability features with a backpropagation neural network. Their model, implemented in a wearable device, achieved an accuracy of 94.35%. The system is lightweight and easy to integrate into safety tools; however, it relies heavily on consistent ECG signal quality, which can be adversely affected by body movement and sensor placement variations. The work of Guo et al. (2025) proposed MMA-Net, which integrates multiple physiological signals, namely EEG, EDA, and PPG, for fatigue detection. By employing attention-based feature extraction modules, the framework achieved strong performance across different time windows. However, the need to acquire and process three heterogeneous signal modalities may introduce practical complexity and computational overhead, limiting its feasibility for real-time in-vehicle deployment.

Yang et al. (2025) proposed an adaptive Multi-Branch CNN model (adMBCNN) that fused handcrafted EEG features with deep functional representations, enabling the model to capture both domain-specific signal characteristics and high-level abstract patterns. By using parallel branches and adaptive fusion, the model mitigates limitations of standard CNNs such as insufficient multi-scale representation and the inability of GCNs to effectively model non-stationary EEG signals, resulting in consistently higher classification accuracy and robustness on multiple public datasets. However, the architectural complexity and increased computational load, arising from multiple branches and feature fusion operations, may restrict its applicability in real-time or resource-constrained embedded driving systems.

To improve model generalizability, Huang et al. (2025) developed a multi-level domain adaptation scheme that performs feature alignment and fusion at both subject and category levels, allowing the model to maintain performance even when evaluated on previously unseen drivers. The experimental results show that the proposed framework achieved an accuracy of 0.942 on the SEED-VIG dataset, indicating strong generalization capability. However, the approach depends on the availability of multiple labelled source datasets, which can be difficult to obtain in real-world driving scenarios due to high annotation costs, privacy concerns, and variability in sensor setups. The work of Wang et al. (2025) focused on improving driver comfort by acquiring ECG signals using semi-dry electrodes. When combined with a wavelet scattering network, the system achieved nearly 98% fatigue detection accuracy while maintaining low processing latency suitable for immediate applications. Although this approach offers a favourable trade-off between comfort and accuracy, it relies solely on ECG information, making it potentially vulnerable to motion artifacts or physiological variability, and does not investigate multimodal fusion, which could enhance robustness rather than merely increasing nominal accuracy.

The study by Liang et al. (2025) introduced FMIF, a vision-based framework employing Convolutional Neural Network (CNN) and Long Short-term Memory (LSTM) layers to jointly model spatial and temporal facial features. The method demonstrated strong performance under varying head poses on the NTHU-DDD dataset. Nevertheless, due to its dependence on clear facial visibility, the approach remains sensitive to occlusions such as hand movements, sunglasses, and poor illumination. The work of Peng et al. (2025) addressed fatigue detection under challenging driving environments such as mountainous roads by enhancing the YOLOv5 object detection framework, a real-time deep learning–based detector, with deformable convolutions, attention mechanisms, and customized loss functions. The proposed model achieved an accuracy of 85% and demonstrated improved robustness to lighting variations and extreme face orientations, though its performance remains inferior compared to scenarios with stable visual conditions. Table 2.4 summarizes the literature discussed above, highlighting the issues considered, the strengths and weaknesses of the approaches adopted.

Table 2.4. Highlights of the literature on driver fatigue detection

Authors	Problem	Solution	Outcome	Limitation
(Anber et al., 2022)	Visual (head, mouth); need for real-time fatigue detection	AlexNet-based CNN and feature extraction with SVM	99.65% accuracy on simulated dataset	No real-world validation
(Karuppusamy and Kang 2020)	EEG, gyroscope, image; lack of multimodal integration	Neural network using hybrid sensor fusion	93.91% detection accuracy	No real-time or field testing
(Arefnezhad et al., 2022)	Behavioural (PERCLOS); fatigue under automation	Simulator-based study on rested/fatigued drivers	Automation reduced effort and workload	Relied on subjective data and simulation
(Dziuda et al., 2021)	Visual (PERCLOS, ECD, FEC); fatigue indicator evaluation	Camera-based detection + FSS questionnaire	PERCLOS and ECD correlated with subjective fatigue	Small sample; simulator-only testing
(Shang et al., 2022)	Visual + emotion; need for combined detection	RM-Xception CNN; time-series fusion of fatigue and emotion indicators	High fatigue accuracy; emotion recognition at 73.32%	Limited emotion accuracy; no real-road tests

Table 2.4. Conti..

(Chen et al., 2022)	Visual (eye closure, yawning); cumulative fatigue modelling	BP neural network with time accumulation and Sigmoid smoothing	Increased accuracy; fewer false detections	Tested only on recorded data
(Xiao et al., 2022)	Visual; dynamic driving fatigue detection	MSFLD with adaptive/statistical thresholds and spatial feature pooling	99.13% accuracy on HNUFDD dataset	No validation under poor lighting or weather
(Chen et al., 2020)	Respiration, heartbeat; limitations of ELM/SVM	DE-ELM using smart bracelet and Doppler radar	Outperformed traditional models	Requires special hardware; lab-only testing
(Dong et al., 2022)	Visual (yawning, eye state, head pose); distraction + fatigue detection	S3FD + FAN + CNN + Random Forest for embedded real-time analysis	Accurate and efficient detection	Handling occlusion and lighting variation not detailed
(Xiang et al., 2022)	Video (grayscale, optical flow); temporal fatigue signals	Multi-branch 3D-CNN with attention + frame aggregation	95% accuracy; improved feature focus	No physiological data integration
(Ye et al., 2021)	Visual (eye, mouth, head pose); false detection due to expressions	RCAN + PnP method for head pose and fatigue detection	>98% accuracy for eye/mouth state	Processing speed and real-time adaptability not explored
(Zhu et al., 2022)	Visual (EAR, MAR, PERCLOS); need for accurate real-time fatigue detection	CNN with 68 facial landmarks and eye/mouth feature extraction	High accuracy and speed; no wearable needed	Focused only on visual input; no physiological signal integration

Table 2.4. Conti…

(Ed-Doughmi et al., 2020)	Visual (facial sequence); detecting fatigue through temporal features	3D CNN + RNN for drowsiness detection using sequential facial frames	Achieved 92% accuracy; real-time suitable	No validation in diverse real-world driving settings
(He et al., 2023)	Passive fatigue; behavioural and physiological response tracking	90-min on-road task with pupil data, gaze, speed and lateral control tracking	Revealed clear passive fatigue patterns	No predictive model developed; limited to one driving condition
(Kassem et al., 2021)	Visual (eye, mouth, head); cost-effective contactless detection	IR camera-based system using facial behaviour cues under various light conditions	93.3% accuracy; worked day and night	Lacked physiological integration; no long-term performance study
(Salvati et al., 2021)	Physiological (HRV); sleepiness detection through pulse rate	HRV-based detection validated against PERCLOS	63% agreement with PERCLOS; useful for continuous monitoring	Small sample size (3 drivers); limited test scenarios
(Sheykhivand et al., 2022)	EEG; need for feature-free, high-speed classification	CNN–LSTM model trained on raw EEG data from 6 brain areas	Outperformed manual-feature models	Requires EEG hardware; may lack in-vehicle usability
(Wang et al., 2021)	EEG; improving fatigue relief through auditory stimulation	VMD-MMSE method with entropy feature extraction + subjective evaluation	Showed reduced fatigue via interesting audio	Not tested over long durations or variable traffic conditions

Table 2.4. Conti…

(Zheng et al., 2023)	Visual (EAR, MAR); robustness under varying environments	MAX-MIN algorithm using ShuffleNet V2K16 + Dlib facial landmarks	98.8% precision; strong performance in real driving	Relied solely on visual cues; physiological data not considered
(He et al., 2024)	Non-visual (PPG, GSR, trip logs); visual fatigue detection too intrusive	Bi-LSTM with attention on real-world truck data	99.21% accuracy; robust and non-intrusive	Focused on truck drivers; generalizability needs testing
(Hu et al., 2024)	EEG; need to improve spatio-temporal fusion	STFN-BRPS model with RMSCM, graph convolution, and attention	Outperformed traditional EEG models in accuracy	High EEG dependence may limit real-time practicality
(Li et al., 2024)	EEG; need for lightweight models on embedded devices	Neural Architecture Search (NAS) created FD-LiteNet	High accuracy with lower computational cost	Real-world robustness under noise not evaluated
(Peng et al., 2024)	Facial video + physiological (multi-source); manual features limiting	Neural network with auto feature fusion	93.15% accuracy in 3s window	Requires synchronized multi-source data
(Tang et al., 2024)	EEG; loss of useful features, overfitting risks	MSCNN-CAM with channel attention	RMSE 0.051, COR 0.966; improved EEG modelling	Cross-subject validation not deeply explored

Table 2.4. Conti…

(Lin et al., 2025)	ECG (HRV); need for portable early detection	BPNN on embedded wearable device	94.35% accuracy; portable & affordable	Sensitive to ECG quality during motion
(Guo, Yang and Wu, 2025)	Multi-modality (EEG, EDA, PPG); cross-subject detection	MMA-Net with SAC-M & attention modules	Strong cross-subject performance	Complex integration of signals required
(Yang et al., 2025)	EEG; single-type models lack adaptability	Adaptive multi-branch CNN (adMBCNN) with handcrafted + functional features	Outperformed existing CNN/GCN models	Complex architecture; may hinder real-time use
(Huang et al., 2025)	EEG; domain shift in cross-subject detection	Multi-Level Domain Adaptation (MLDA) using improved Wasserstein distance	Accuracy: 0.942 (SEED-VIG), 0.843 (SADT)	Requires labelled multi-subject data for training
(Wang, Chen and Zhang, 2025)	ECG; traditional electrodes inconvenient	Semi-dry electrode + wavelet scattering network	97.93% accuracy; real-time capability	Focused on ECG alone; lacks multimodal context
(Liang et al., 2025)	Visual (face); pose change and motion sensitivity	FMIF with spatial-temporal fusion (CNN + LSTM)	Strong results on NTHU-DDD dataset	Sensitive to lighting/occlusion
(Peng et al., 2025)	Visual under complex road (mountain); lighting impact	YOLOv5 + deformable conv, triplet attention, Wing loss	85% accuracy in poor visual settings	Lower than state-of-the-art; real-time tuning needed

2.4. REVIEW OF STUDIES ON DRIVER'S DROWSINESS DETECTION

The recent advances in the field of driver drowsiness detection include a variety of techniques proposed by researchers, ranging from image processing, machine learning, physiological monitoring to hybrid and edge-based systems. The work conducted by (Albadawi et al., 2023) introduced a contactless real-time system to detect drowsiness by capturing facial features through a camera mounted on the dashboard. The system extracts key indicators such as EAR, MAR, head posture, etc., and achieves an accuracy rate of up to 99% on the NTHU dataset. Its main advantages are fast response time and no need for physical sensors. However, because it relies solely on visual input, performance may degrade in low light or when the camera's field of view is obstructed. Also focusing on visual cues, Altameem et al. (2021) explored the use of facial expressions for sleepiness and emotion recognition through a hybrid model integrated into an in-vehicle system. The system employed SVMs to classify driver emotions and trigger warning alerts in potentially dangerous situations. Despite achieving 83.25% accuracy under varying lighting conditions, the proposed approach remains relatively basic compared to recent deep learning–based methods and is limited to facial information alone.

To improve comfort and wear resistance (i.e., the ability of wearable sensors to remain reliable and stable during prolonged use without causing discomfort or signal degradation), Amidei et al. (2023) proposed a fatigue detection model based on Skin Conductance (SC) signals acquired from a wristband. The study evaluated three ensemble learning techniques, namely Bagging, Boosting, and Stacking, among which the Boosting-based classifier achieved the best performance with an accuracy of 89.4%. The results indicate that a single, minimally intrusive wearable sensor can be effective for sleepiness detection; however, the absence of behavioural or visual cues limits the robustness of the system under diverse driving conditions.

Addressing this limitation, Bajaj et al. (2023) combined facial information and physiological signals for fatigue detection. Their framework employed Multi-task Cascaded Convolutional Neural Networks (MTCNN) for face detection along with a Galvanic Skin Response (GSR) sensor to enhance detection accuracy across different driving scenarios. Although the model achieved 91% accuracy in simulated environments, it was not validated under real-world driving conditions, raising concerns regarding its practical effectiveness.

Similarly, Esteves et al. (2021) proposed a more personalized fatigue detection strategy by integrating ECG signals and facial features within an immersive driving simulator. The study recognized that drivers exhibit individual-specific drowsiness patterns and introduced a customized learning mechanism tailored to each driver. While this personalized framework is not yet suitable for real-time deployment, it highlights the importance of individual adaptation, which is conceptually reused in this thesis, whereas simulator-dependent data acquisition and personalized calibration requirements are not adopted due to deployment constraints.

Ebrahimian et al. (2022) developed a deep learning framework that combined ECG and respiratory signals to classify multiple levels of driver sleepiness. Their CNN–LSTM model achieved 91% accuracy for three-class classification, corresponding to alert, mildly drowsy, and highly drowsy states, but only 67% accuracy for five-class detection, where finer-grained sleepiness levels were considered. Although five-class classification enables detailed fatigue analysis, such performance degradation is less critical in practical driving scenarios, where the primary requirement is reliable discrimination between alert and drowsy states. Despite its effectiveness in modelling physiological variations, the model's architectural complexity and multimodal signal processing requirements may hinder real-time deployment in in-vehicle systems.

The work of Florez et al. (2023) focused on real-time fatigue detection using only the eye region, evaluating three deep learning architectures. ResNet50V2 achieved the best performance with an accuracy of 99.71% on the NITYMED dataset. [NITYMED: Near-Infrared Tirelessness Monitoring Eye Dataset]. While the model is computationally efficient and highly accurate, its reliance solely on ocular features ignores complementary physiological and behavioural indicators of sleepiness. Similarly, Jahan et al. (2023) investigated eye-based fatigue cues and proposed a CNN architecture termed "4D", which predicts driver sleepiness by analysing eye states using the MRL Eye Dataset. The proposed model outperformed conventional CNN architectures such as VGG16 and VGG19, achieving an accuracy of 97.53%. However, the approach was evaluated only under controlled conditions, and the absence of testing across diverse driving environments and lighting variations may limit its generalizability in real-world applications.

To improve accessibility in the transport sector, Khan et al. (2023) designed an IoT-based system operating across edge and cloud platforms. The model uses video-based analytics to detect fatigue, yawning, and distraction, and provides real-time alerts through an Android application. Although it achieved 96% accuracy, the system requires stable network connectivity and supporting infrastructure for reliable operation. Lamaazi et al. (2023) extended this idea through a two-stage framework emphasizing privacy and efficiency. The first stage employs a CNN to analyse facial cues locally, while the second stage integrates YOLOv5 (You Only Look Once v5) and an LSTM network for temporal fatigue analysis. While this design improves efficiency and privacy, it remains dependent on visual data quality and network coordination, which may limit robustness in real-world conditions.

YOLOv5 is further used to examine the vehicle's motion patterns, and drowsiness is confirmed only when both visual and vehicle-based cues are consistent. Despite achieving 97.7% accuracy, large-scale deployment of edge computing devices can be challenging due to hardware costs, installation complexity, maintenance requirements, and the need for reliable power and connectivity across fleets. Li et al. (2023) adopted a novel approach by embedding a lightweight CNN into a wearable smart-glasses prototype to measure blinking frequency. Using thermal lenses, the camera is discreetly mounted on the glasses, providing blink detection performance comparable to commercial eye-tracking systems while preserving privacy and real-world usability. However, reliance on custom-designed wearable hardware may limit cost-effectiveness, user adoption, and scalability.

Savas and Becerikli (2020) presented a real-time fatigue detection method using a multi-task Convolutional Neural Network (ConNN) that simultaneously analyzed eye and mouth features. By computing metrics such as PERCLOS and frequency of mouth opening (FOM), the model classified driver fatigue into three levels, namely alert, moderately fatigued, and severely fatigued states. Tested on publicly available datasets including YawDD and NTHU-DDD, the framework achieved an accuracy of 98.81%. The study is notable for jointly integrating two complementary facial fatigue indicators within a single model. However, the approach remains entirely vision-based, making it vulnerable to lighting variations, facial occlusions, and camera positioning issues. The work of Murata et al. (2022) examined whether a PERCLOS threshold of 70% (PERCLOS70) is effective for drowsiness assessment in a driving simulator. The authors observed that PERCLOS70 values increased consistently with rising drowsiness levels and showed strong agreement with Karolinska

Sleepiness Scale (KSS) subjective ratings, indicating that PERCLOS70 reliably reflects prolonged eye closure associated with fatigue. Despite these encouraging results, the evaluation was limited to simulated driving conditions, and no real-world validation was performed.

Similarly, Ngxande et al. (2020) addressed racial bias in vision-based drowsiness detection systems by proposing a framework based on Generative Adversarial Networks (GANs). The GAN model was used to synthetically generate facial images representing underrepresented ethnic groups, thereby augmenting existing datasets. A CNN retrained on the augmented dataset demonstrated improved detection accuracy and reduced performance disparity across ethnicities, highlighting the importance of dataset diversity. However, the approach is computationally intensive, requires careful validation of synthetic data quality, and remains restricted to visual modalities, limiting its robustness in non-ideal sensing conditions. Paulo et al. (2021) introduced a zero-calibration EEG-based drowsiness detection framework, in which EEG signals were transformed into image representations such as recurrence plots and Gramian angular fields and classified using convolutional neural networks. The system achieved a balanced accuracy of 75.87% across 27 subjects using leave-one-out validation, demonstrating the feasibility of subject-independent EEG-based fatigue detection. However, the performance remained inferior to vision-based methods, and the requirement for complex EEG acquisition hardware limits its practicality for real-world driving applications. In a similar direction, Sunagawa et al. (2020) proposed a fatigue detection approach that combined eye blinking behaviour and driver posture features to identify different drowsiness stages ranging from mild to severe. Using simulator data collected from approximately 50 drivers, the method showed improved sensitivity in detecting early-stage (weak) drowsiness. Although the system is lightweight and suitable for in-vehicle integration, its reported performance metrics such as moderate F1-score (classification reliability) and RMSE (prediction error magnitude), were limited, and the approach was not validated under real-world driving conditions.

Vijaypriya and Uma (2023) proposed a robust fatigue detection framework based on a Multi-Scale Convolutional Neural Network (MCNN). Their approach employed hybrid wavelet-based feature extraction and parameter optimization using the Flamingo Search Algorithm (FSA). The model achieved over 98% accuracy on both the YawDD and NTHU-DDD datasets, significantly outperforming conventional methods. However, the framework relies exclusively on visual cues and would benefit from evaluation in uncontrolled or real-world driving environments.

Zhang et al. (2022) developed a privacy-preserving drowsiness detection system based on federated transfer learning, enabling multiple edge devices to collaboratively train a shared model without exchanging raw driver data. This design preserves data privacy while maintaining reliable detection performance. Nevertheless, the approach depends on stable network connectivity and hardware standardization across edge devices, which may hinder large-scale deployment. The work of Maheswari et al. (2022) introduced an integrated vision-based system that computed eye aspect ratio (EAR), mouth aspect ratio (MAR), and PERCLOS, and further proposed a new descriptor termed Facial Aspect Ratio (FAR). The model was capable of detecting complex fatigue-related behaviours, including yawning, head nodding, and face-covering gestures, and demonstrated robustness to head pose variations, sunglasses, and partial facial occlusions. Evaluated on multiple public datasets, the system achieved strong performance, with reported accuracy exceeding 95%, though the absence of physiological signal integration limits its potential for further accuracy enhancement. There are also recent studies adopting advanced and hybrid approaches, such as the work of Madni et al. (2024), which introduced a drowsiness detection framework based on eye-movement analysis using transfer learning. The authors combined VGG-16 (a 16-layer deep convolutional neural network originally designed for large-scale image recognition) with a Light Gradient-Boosting Machine (LGBM) classifier to form a hybrid model termed VGLG. The framework extracted discriminative spatial features from eye images and achieved 99% detection accuracy with an inference time below 0.009 s. Although the system demonstrates excellent speed and precision, its exclusive reliance on ocular cues limits robustness under occlusion or poor illumination, rather than overall detection accuracy.

Similarly, Das et al. (2024) proposed a non-intrusive drowsiness detection system combining CNN–LSTM with a U-Net architecture (an encoder–decoder network widely used for fine-grained feature localization in images). The model analysed facial motion patterns from video sequences and was evaluated using multiple CNN backbones, including VGG16, ResNet50, and MobileNet, for feature extraction. The CNN–LSTM configuration yielded the best performance, and the authors reported its suitability for Advanced Driver Assistance Systems (ADAS) due to its temporal modelling capability and real-time feasibility, as demonstrated through experimental evaluation. Alguindigue et al. (2024) proposed an EEG-based drowsiness detection framework using deep neural networks optimized through Teaching–Learning-Based Optimization (TLBO) and Student Psychology-Based Optimization (SPBO). TLBO is a population-based metaheuristic inspired by the knowledge transfer between teachers and learners, aiming to reduce model complexity while improving convergence, whereas SPBO mimics student learning behaviours such as imitation and competition to accelerate training speed. Both optimization strategies improved classification performance, with TLBO producing a more compact network structure and SPBO enabling faster convergence. The models achieved strong predictive performance (AUC > 0.92); however, SPBO exhibited slight overfitting, particularly in the presence of atypical EEG patterns such as abrupt amplitude spikes, motion-induced artifacts, or subject-specific baseline shifts, which affected generalization. Moreover, the exclusive dependence on EEG signals reduces practical feasibility, as EEG acquisition requires specialized hardware, careful electrode placement, and is sensitive to noise and user discomfort, limiting large-scale or everyday in-vehicle deployment.

Given that a large portion of the reviewed literature relies on EEG signals, it is important to note that although EEG offers high sensitivity to cognitive fatigue, its practicality in everyday driving is consistently constrained by hardware complexity and user comfort requirements. In this context, Jebraeily et al. (2024) enhanced CNN performance for EEG-based drowsiness detection by optimizing the network architecture using a genetic algorithm, which adaptively selected model parameters to better capture temporal dependencies in EEG signals. While the optimized model showed improved accuracy in learning complex EEG patterns, it required substantial computational resources and was not validated in real-world driving conditions, limiting its deployment feasibility.

Similarly, Yadav et al. (2025) proposed an EEG-based framework using only six EEG channels, combining short-time Fourier transform (STFT), which converts non-stationary EEG signals into time–frequency representations, with an Inception-based CNN (a multi-branch convolutional architecture designed to capture features at different receptive field scales) enhanced by self-attention mechanisms. This design helped preserve temporal information and reduce signal loss during feature extraction. The model achieved a moderate accuracy of 79.02%, indicating effective large-scale EEG processing; however, such performance suggests that further refinement is necessary before adoption in safety-critical driving applications, where higher reliability is required.

Lee et al. (2025) conducted a comparative study using eye image–based learning models, evaluating both ML and DL approaches. Among the classifiers tested, K-Nearest Neighbors (KNN), a conventional ML algorithm, achieved 98.89% accuracy, while YOLOv5 and YOLOv8 demonstrated superior performance in facial feature localization. The study highlighted the complementary strengths of ML classifiers for decision making and deep learning–based computer vision models for feature extraction in drowsiness detection. However, the framework depends on clear facial visibility, which may limit performance under adverse visual conditions.

Similarly, Essahraui et al. (2025) proposed a hybrid system combining machine learning and computer vision for detecting eye and mouth states. YOLOv5 and YOLOv8 achieved near-perfect precision and recall on benchmark datasets, outperforming Faster R-CNN, which is known for higher computational cost and slower inference speed. While the system demonstrated strong performance, real-time operation here refers to low-latency inference capable of processing video frames at driving-compatible frame rates, and the approach still relies entirely on camera input, making it sensitive to poor illumination and facial occlusions.

In another work, Arava and Sundaram (2025) developed a drowsiness detection system using fuzzy logic combined with an enhanced Viola–Jones algorithm, a classical object detection method based on Haar-like features and cascade classifiers for rapid face and eye detection. The model achieved 97.5% accuracy and functioned effectively under both daytime and nighttime conditions, including for drivers wearing glasses. Despite its strong real-time responsiveness, the image-only design may overlook subtle physiological fatigue indicators such as heart rate variability or micro-changes in skin conductance that are not visually observable. Table 2.5 highlights the insight drawn from the above discussed literature.

Table 2.5. Highlights of the above discussed literature on driver drowsiness detection

Authors	Problem	Solution	Outcome	Limitation
(Albadawi et al., 2023)	Visual (EAR, MAR, head pose); need for real-time non-invasive detection	Dashboard camera + facial landmarks + 3 classifiers	Up to 99% accuracy; fast alert system	May be affected by lighting and camera angles
(Altameem et al., 2021)	Visual; emotion + drowsiness detection under variable lighting	SVM-based facial expression monitoring integrated with vehicle electronics	83.25% accuracy; detects unsafe emotional states	Moderate performance; limited to facial input
(Amidei et al., 2023)	Physiological (skin conductance); wearable-only detection	Wrist SC signals + ensemble algorithms (Boosting best)	89.4% accuracy; comfortable and lightweight system	Lacks behavioural signal integration
(Bajaj et al., 2023)	Visual + physiological; single-signal limits accuracy	Hybrid model using MTCNN (face) + GSR sensor (SC)	91% efficacy; detects transition to drowsy state	Simulated environment only; no field validation
(Esteves et al., 2021)	ECG + facial data; individual variability in drowsiness	Subject-specific models via machine learning and immersive simulation	Personalized detection framework proposed	Real-world deployment not explored
(Ebrahimian et al., 2022)	ECG + respiration; multi-level fatigue detection	CNN and CNN–LSTM with HRV, PSD and respiration input	CNN–LSTM: 91% (3-level) and 67% (5-level) accuracy	Complex model; real-time performance and deployment not tested

Table 2.5. Conti..

(Florez et al., 2023)	Visual (eye region); drowsiness via blink detection	CNN models (ResNet50V2, InceptionV3, VGG16) on NITYMED dataset	ResNet50V2 reached 99.71% accuracy	Focused only on eyes; lacks multi-modal integration
(Jahan et al., 2023)	Visual (eye state); fast eye state prediction	Novel 4D CNN compared with VGG16 and VGG19 on MRL Eye dataset	97.53% accuracy; outperformed existing models	Controlled data only; no test in diverse driving conditions
(Khan et al., 2023)	Visual; IoT-based real-time system for transport safety	Edge + cloud + mobile app; CV detects yawns, sleep, distraction	96% accuracy; scalable and portable system	Needs stable network and system integration
(Lamaazi et al., 2023)	Visual + vehicle motion; privacy-aware edge-based detection	Smart edge system using CNN + YoLov5 + LSTM fusion	97.7% accuracy; ensures user privacy	High system complexity; edge device capacity may limit application
(Li et al., 2023)	Visual (blink rate); non-intrusive wearable glasses	Hot-mirror camera + lightweight CNN for blink detection	Blink rate matched eye-tracker standard	Needs specialized hardware (smart glasses)
(Savas and Becerikli, 2020)	Visual (eye, mouth); need for multi-input fatigue classification	Multi-task ConNN classifying PERCLOS & FOM simultaneously	98.81% accuracy on YawDD and NTHU-DDD	Model tested only on visual input under specific conditions

Table 2.5. Conti…

(Murata, Doi and Karwowski, 2022)	Visual (PERCLOS); assessing PERCLOS70 for drowsiness prediction	Simulator-based validation of PERCLOS70 using KSS correlation	Validated PERCLOS70 as reliable drowsiness indicator	No real-world data; limited to simulated experiments
N(gxande, Tapamo and Burke, 2020)	Visual + dataset bias; models underperform on diverse races	GAN-based augmentation to improve CNN detection across ethnicity	Improved fairness and detection accuracy	High computational cost; limited to visual domain
(Paulo, Pires and Nunes, 2021)	EEG; need for cross-subject, zero-calibration detection	Recurrence plots and GAF encoding + CNN classification of EEG data	75.87% accuracy with leave-one-out validation	EEG signal complexity; lower accuracy than visual models
(Sunagawa et al., 2020)	Visual + behavioral (blink, posture); covering full drowsiness stages	Model combining posture + eye info for weak and strong drowsiness detection	Covered all stages; improved weak-stage detection	Moderate F1-score (53.6%); no field testing
(Vijaypriya and Uma, 2023)	Visual; enhance facial-based drowsiness recognition	MCNN with hybrid features and Flamingo Search optimization	~98.3% accuracy on NTHU-DDD and YawDD	No physiological input; tested only in controlled datasets
(Zhang et al.. 2022)	Visual + privacy concerns in model training	Federated transfer learning to enable privacy-aware model training across devices	Maintained accuracy while preserving user data privacy	Depends on strong network and compatible edge devices

Table 2.5. Conti..

(Madni et al., 2024)	Visual (eye movement); discomfort from contact-based systems	Transfer learning approach using VGG-16 + LGBM (VGLG) with k-NN classification	Achieved 99% accuracy; detection speed of 0.00829s	Focused only on eye features; lacked multimodal input
(Das et al., 2024)	Visual (facial movement); need for real-time, non-intrusive detection	CNN-LSTM model with U-Net-based architecture on various deep learning models	CNN-LSTM showed superior accuracy and real-time capability	May face issues under poor lighting or facial occlusion
(Alguindigue et al., 2024)	EEG (physiological); optimization challenges in DNNs	CNN architecture optimized using TLBO and SPBO meta-heuristic algorithms	AUC > 0.92; SPBO faster, TLBO simpler	EEG acquisition complexity; minor overfitting in SPBO
(Jebraeily et al., 2024)	EEG; training inefficiency with standard CNNs	CNN optimization using a genetic algorithm to improve architecture	Enhanced detection of drowsiness with optimized model	Requires high computing power; lacks real-world testing
(Yadav et al., 2025)	EEG; high-dimensional signals with info loss	STFT + self-attention mechanism in Inception model using 6 EEG channels	79.02% accuracy; minimized info loss	Moderate accuracy; requires high-quality EEG data

2.5 FINDINGS AND OPEN RESEARCH ISSUES

A critical analysis of the existing literature reveals several dominant research trends in the area of driver drowsiness detection. Recent studies increasingly rely on artificial intelligence–based techniques, particularly deep learning models, due to their strong capability in extracting discriminative facial and behavioral features related to fatigue and vigilance degradation. Image-based approaches have emerged as the most practical solutions because of their non-intrusive nature and ease of integration into modern vehicles, whereas physiological and vehicle-based methods are often constrained by sensor intrusiveness, hardware complexity, or dependency on driving context. At the same time, many studies continue to prioritize high classification accuracy under controlled or simulated conditions, often at the expense of real-time feasibility, robustness, and interpretability. Furthermore, a large portion of the literature treats drowsiness as a binary state and performs classification on isolated frames, despite strong evidence from subjective sleepiness scales and behavioral studies that drowsiness evolves gradually and manifests through continuous temporal patterns. These trends highlight a growing gap between algorithmic performance reported in research environments and the practical requirements of real-world driver monitoring systems. Based on the above review, the key research gaps identified in the literature are summarized as follows:

- Many deep learning–based systems exhibit high computational complexity, which limits their suitability for real-time deployment on resource-constrained in-vehicle or embedded platforms.
- Existing image-based approaches show reduced robustness under varying illumination conditions, nighttime driving, facial occlusions such as glasses or masks, and changes in driver posture or head pose.
- A significant number of studies rely exclusively on either physiological signals or visual cues, without effectively integrating complementary behavioral indicators to improve reliability.
- Most proposed systems model driver drowsiness as a binary classification problem, ignoring its gradual progression and intermediate vigilance states.

- Temporal continuity and contextual relationships across video frames are often neglected, leading to unstable predictions and frequent false alerts.
- Inter-individual variability related to age, gender, facial structure, and physiological response is rarely addressed, limiting generalization across diverse driver populations.
- Very few approaches achieve an effective balance between lightweight design, interpretability, and high detection accuracy suitable for real-world use.

The research presented in this thesis is explicitly designed to address these gaps through a multi-stage and context-aware framework. Instead of relying on a single detection mechanism, the proposed approach incrementally combines lightweight deep learning–based appearance analysis, robust behavioral cue extraction using a hybrid CNN–SVM strategy, and adaptive fuzzy logic–based decision making. By modeling drowsiness as a continuous process rather than a binary event, the proposed system enables stable multi-level vigilance classification and reduces false alarms. The framework prioritizes real-time robustness and interpretability over isolated offline accuracy, with performance evaluated using live video streams under diverse conditions. This design philosophy directly responds to the limitations identified in existing studies and positions the proposed work as a practical and deployable solution for real-world driver drowsiness monitoring.

2.6 SUMMARY

This chapter presented a structured review of recent research on driver monitoring systems for attention, fatigue, and drowsiness detection. The survey covered a wide range of approaches, including physiological, vehicle-based, and image-based methods, with a primary focus on identifying dominant research trends and practical limitations rather than providing exhaustive analysis of individual techniques. The literature indicates that although many studies report high detection accuracy, performance is often evaluated under controlled or simulated conditions, which limits reproducibility and real-world reliability. Among the reviewed approaches, image-based deep learning methods are the most widely adopted due to their non-intrusive nature and ease of integration into modern vehicles without requiring wearable sensors or vehicle modifications. In contrast, physiological approaches based on EEG or ECG offer high sensitivity but remain impractical for everyday driving because of hardware intrusiveness and user acceptance issues, whereas vehicle-based techniques are strongly influenced by driving style and road conditions. Although deep learning models are computationally demanding, advances in embedded hardware, model compression, and optimized inference increasingly support real-time deployment. The review reveals that many existing systems treat drowsiness as a binary event and perform classification on isolated frames, despite evidence that fatigue and drowsiness develop gradually over time. Limited attention is given to temporal continuity, adaptive decision making, and clear differentiation between fatigue and drowsiness as distinct cognitive states. In addition, robustness under varying illumination, facial occlusion, and long-duration driving remains insufficiently addressed. The findings directly motivate the proposed research, which prioritizes i) non-intrusive facial analysis, ii) gradual multi-level vigilance modeling, and iii) computationally efficient architectures suitable for real-time in-vehicle deployment. The subsequent chapters build upon these insights to develop a lightweight and context-aware driver drowsiness detection framework.

CHAPTER-3

DEEP LEARNING FRAMEWORK FOR DRIVER DROWSINESS PREDICTION BASED ON EYE STATE

3.1 INTRODUCTION

This chapter presents the first contribution of the research work, which emphasizes the development of an effective predictive model using a deep learning approach for detecting drowsiness based on eye state classification. The reason behind considering eye state is that it is one of the major and direct indicators of drowsiness, which can be linked to the fact that while driving, if the eye remains closed for a certain duration, say more than one second, it can be considered a sign of drowsiness or the onset of a micro-sleep. Although multi-feature approaches are widely discussed and critically analyzed in the previous chapter, this study deliberately focuses on eye state in order to establish a robust and reliable eye-based detection model, which can later serve as a foundation for integrating additional indicators. Under normal conditions, a typical human blink (or the temporary closure of both eyes) generally lasts for about one-third of a second. This observation is supported by several studies in the context of human behavior and cognitive fatigue, which have reported that prolonged eye closure, frequent blinking, or abnormally slow blink rates are strong physiological markers of drowsiness (Horne and Reyner, 1999; Sahayadhas et al., 2012; Murata et al., 2022). Therefore, efficient monitoring and classification of eye state are considered essential for the early detection of drowsiness, which can support timely alert generation and contribute to the prevention of road accidents.

In the proposed framework, multiple deep learning models based on different CNN architectures are implemented and systematically evaluated on a custom dataset of facial images containing diverse environmental conditions and scene variations. The use of a custom dataset is motivated by the limitations observed in many publicly available datasets, which often lack sufficient diversity in terms of illumination, facial accessories, pose variations, and real-world visual complexity, as discussed in the previous chapter. By constructing a dataset that better reflects unconstrained driving scenarios, the study aims to improve model generalization and practical applicability. In the initial phase, several deep learning models are preselected based on their architectural characteristics and prior adoption in related vision-based classification tasks. Each model is then analyzed in terms of its strengths and weaknesses with respect to eye-state-based drowsiness detection, considering both predictive performance and computational efficiency. Based on this structured evaluation, the most suitable model is identified and subsequently fine-tuned through targeted optimization to further enhance its robustness and reliability.

3.2 PROBLEM DESCRIPTION

Based on the critical analysis of existing studies, it is evident that the primary challenge in driver drowsiness detection does not lie in the lack of proposed methods, but rather in achieving reliable, adaptive, and real-time detection performance under diverse and unconstrained driving conditions. The prior research has explored a wide range of solutions, broadly categorized into invasive approaches such as those relying on physiological signals including heart rate, steering behavior, and EEG and non-invasive approaches based on visual cues and image processing techniques. While invasive methods often provide high sensitivity, their dependency on specialized sensors, cost, and limited practicality restrict their large-scale adoption in ordinary vehicles, especially when real-time deployment and user comfort are considered.

Non-invasive approaches, particularly those based on rule-driven image processing and classical machine learning techniques, have therefore gained attention due to their unobtrusive nature. However, many of these methods rely heavily on hand-crafted feature extraction and heuristic rules, which makes them vulnerable to variations in illumination, head pose, facial appearance, and occlusion. As a result, their performance often degrades significantly when exposed to real-world driving scenarios involving inter-subject variability and dynamic environmental conditions. With the emergence of DL, CNN architecture has been increasingly adopted for drowsiness-related tasks due to their ability to automatically learn discriminative features from raw image data. CNN-based methods have demonstrated promising results for visual cues such as eye state and yawning detection. Nevertheless, a closer examination of existing CNN-based studies reveals two critical gaps: first, many approaches rely on limited or highly controlled datasets that lack sufficient subject and environmental diversity; and second, pre-trained models are often adopted without a systematic evaluation of their suitability for eye state–specific classification tasks. Moreover, there is a lack of comprehensive comparative analysis across different CNN architectures, particularly with respect to balancing classification accuracy against computational efficiency, which is a key requirement for real-time in-vehicle deployment. To address these gaps, this chapter does not restrict itself solely to dataset preparation but instead presents a structured investigation of an eye state–based deep learning framework. The chapter encompasses the construction of a diverse facial image dataset, the implementation and comparative evaluation of multiple CNN architectures, and the identification and fine-tuning of the most suitable model. The objective is to establish a robust and computationally efficient eye state classification framework that can serve as a reliable building block for real-time driver drowsiness detection systems, while also enabling future integration with additional behavioral or physiological indicators.

3.3 PROPOSED FRAMEWORK DESIGN

This section explains the design of the proposed framework and outlines the technical modules and methodological steps followed to develop a reliable and computationally efficient prediction model for driver drowsiness detection using eye-state information extracted from facial images. The main aim of this framework is to offer a non-intrusive approach that identifies early drowsiness symptoms under practical driving conditions, where changes in illumination, facial pose, and individual appearance can significantly affect visual cues. In addition to this, the framework focuses on reducing the tendency of the predictive model toward overfitting and incorrect alarms, where a false-positive case represents an alert driver that is mistakenly detected as drowsy, without compromising overall accuracy or real-time applicability. The complete structural flow of the proposed framework is presented in Figure 3.1, which shows the interaction between each processing stage and the final decision module.

The first component of the proposed framework focuses on the preparation of a custom facial image dataset consisting of images of both male and female subjects collected from Google Images, Kaggle repositories, and other online sources. Since the images are gathered from heterogeneous sources, they inherently exhibit variations in resolution, pose, illumination, and facial accessories. This motivates the use of a custom dataset to explicitly incorporate such variability, which is often limited or controlled in existing benchmark datasets, thereby supporting better generalization in real-world driving scenarios.

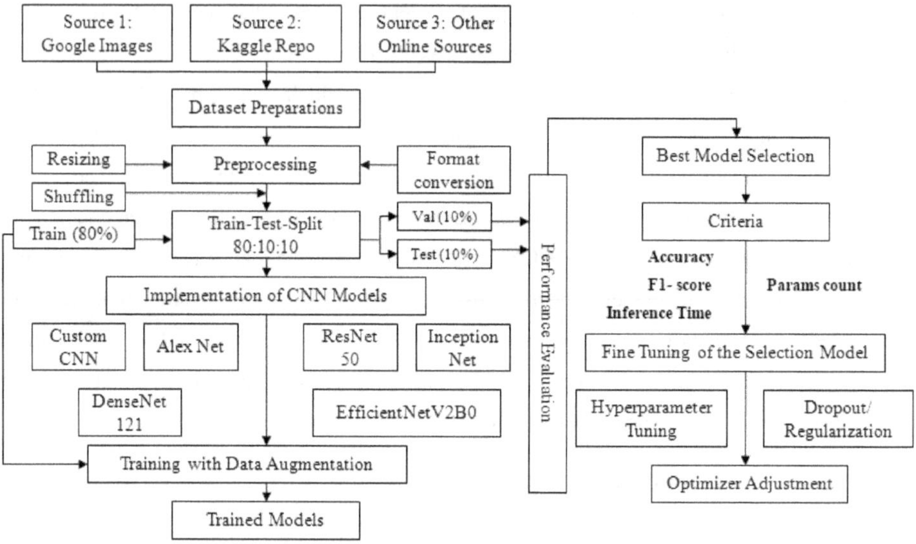

Figure 3.1. Schematic Illustration of the proposed framework

To maintain uniformity and suitability for effective model learning, the subsequent module performs dataset preprocessing, which covers image resizing, format standardization, and random sample reordering. Each image is converted into a fixed dimensional structure so that it remains compatible with convolutional neural network input requirements and avoids shape-related inconsistencies during training. Furthermore, the complete dataset is partitioned into three subsets using an 80:10:10 ratio that corresponds to training, validation, and testing data, respectively. The validation subset supports hyperparameter adjustment and model selection decisions, whereas the testing subset remains isolated and is used only for unbiased assessment of the final model performance.

The next stage of the proposed framework focuses on the implementation of multiple convolutional neural network architectures, which include a conventional CNN model along with widely used pre-trained networks such as AlexNet (Krizhevsky et al.), VGG16 (Simonyan and Zisserman), ResNet50 (He et al.), InceptionV3 (Szegedy et al.), DenseNet121 (Huang et al.), and EfficientNetV2B0 (Tan and Le). These architectures were selected because earlier image classification studies frequently applied them and reported consistent performance across diverse visual recognition tasks, thereby making them suitable candidates for comparative analysis in this study. Model training uses only the predefined training dataset to maintain strict data separation. To improve robustness against real-world variations, data augmentation strategies such as rotation, flipping, and scaling are applied to the training samples so that the models handle changes in orientation, size, and appearance more effectively during practical deployment.

Once the training process is completed, all implemented models undergo evaluation using commonly accepted performance measures such as accuracy, precision, recall, and F1-score, where accuracy and F1-score receive primary emphasis for judging overall classification capability. Along with predictive performance, inference time and the total count of trainable parameters are also examined in order to analyze computational efficiency and deployment feasibility, which remain essential requirements for real-time in-vehicle applications. Based on this structured comparative evaluation, the most appropriate CNN architecture is identified and further improved through fine-tuning procedures that include dropout regularization, learning rate modification, and optimizer selection, thereby maintaining a balance between classification accuracy and practical real-time usability.

3.3.1 Dataset Preparation

Establishing a robust dataset is an important aspect of deep learning–based systems, particularly when the objective involves classification of human behavioral states such as driver drowsiness. Although multiple publicly available datasets exist for eye state and drowsiness analysis, their applicability is often constrained by controlled acquisition settings, limited subject diversity, or restricted environmental variations, which reduces their suitability for evaluating robustness under practical driving conditions. For this reason, a tailored dataset was assembled to better align with the requirements of real-world eye-state–based drowsiness detection. The constructed dataset was designed to address common limitations observed in existing resources, such as imbalanced sample distributions, lack of contextual variability, and dependence on laboratory-like capture conditions. The primary objective was to assemble facial images that more closely resemble realistic operational scenarios encountered during driving, thereby supporting improved generalization across diverse conditions. The dataset construction process focused on preserving natural variations in appearance and environment, while excluding only clearly irrelevant samples unrelated to the driving or vigilance context.

After preprocessing, the final dataset comprised approximately 10,000 facial images, evenly distributed across two eye-state classes, namely active state (eyes open) and drowsy state (eyes closed), with roughly 5,000 samples per class. Special attention was given to incorporating variability within the dataset, including differences in illumination, facial orientation, accessories, and partial occlusions. Approximately 34% of the images include subjects wearing glasses, 12% include facial masks, and 28% are captured under low-light or night-time conditions, ensuring that the dataset reflects practical challenges encountered in real-world deployment scenarios. A reference summary of the dataset composition and sources is provided in Table 3.1.

Table 3.1. A highlight of operation considered in custom dataset creation process

Step	Description
Identifying Limitations	Initial review showed that most available datasets lacked diversity and had limited real-world coverage.
Web Scraping	We collected over 6,000 photos from Google and Bing using keywords such as "drowsy driver", "active driver", "awake person", "drowsy person", "active driver wearing a mask", and "drowsy motorist wearing a mask".
Enhancing with Kaggle Data	We have added ~12,000 labelled images from existing Kaggle repositories (Jebraeily, et al., 2024) related to eye state and drowsiness.
Manual Review and Refinement	The dataset is manually reviewed and filtered out irrelevant or duplicate images, finalizing ~10,000 high-quality samples.
Ensuring Diversity	Images were chosen to represent different lighting, angles, and facial conditions for better generalization.
Final Dataset Composition	The final dataset consists of approximately 10,000 images, balanced between active and drowsy classes, enhancing the model's ability to generalize and improving accuracy and reliability.

Figure 3.2 presents sample images from the proposed custom-made dataset, covering diverse visual conditions associated with both alert and drowsy eye states. While not all images are captured inside a vehicle cabin, this design choice intentionally introduces

variability in illumination, facial pose, and occlusion, which is essential for learning robust eye-state features independent of background context. The dataset is primarily used to train the eye-state classification model, whereas real-time in-vehicle images are employed during testing and validation to assess practical driving performance.

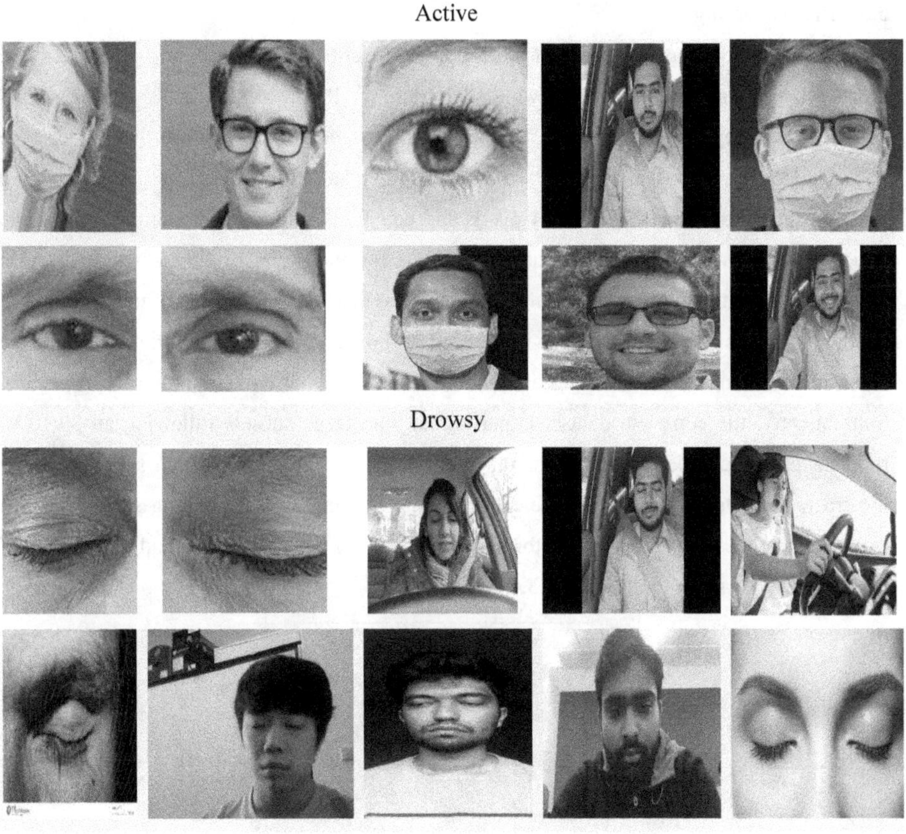

Figure 3.2. Sample visualization of the custom dataset prepared in the proposed work

Figure 3.2 gives an image of the diversity incorporated into the proposed custom dataset. The active class features people whose eyes are open, with an apparent state of being alert, with variation in facial accessories, illumination, and whether or not their varied angles. The sleepy class produced pictures of subjects with visible signs of tiredness as indicated by closed eyes, sagging eyelids, and non-attentive faces. Apart from fatigue cues, facial accessories and surrounding conditions introduce additional variability to the image set. This variability is valuable because it will enable the model to learn differences in eye state and facial cues in a more heterogeneous population and variability in conditions. When the model is trained on such a varied dataset, it will be better able to recognize drowsiness in real-world scenarios which is a necessity for real-world driver monitoring systems.

3.3.2 Preprocessing

The second major stage of the framework applies a series of preprocessing operations that prepare the image data for effective model training. Preprocessing acts as an essential normalization step so that the neural network receives standardized inputs during the learning phase and avoids inconsistencies caused by data source variation. All images are resized to a fixed spatial resolution of 224 × 224 pixels and converted into an RGB-normalized format, which represents the common input requirement for most convolutional neural network architectures. This uniform representation ensures that images captured under different conditions exhibit consistent behavior during training. In order to eliminate sequence-dependent learning bias, the images are randomly shuffled before the training process begins. Subsequently, the complete dataset is partitioned into three subsets following an 80:10:10 ratio for training, validation, and testing, respectively, where the validation subset supports hyperparameter tuning and model selection during training, and the testing subset remains isolated for final and unbiased performance evaluation. The allocation and proportion of these subsets are shown in Figures 3.3, 3.4, and 3.5.

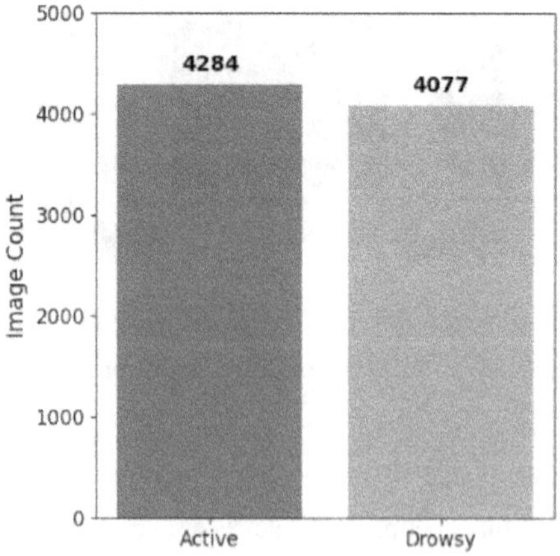

Figure 3.3. Training set distribution

The Figure 3.3 represents the training set data distribution, and it can be observed that there are 4,284 active and 4,077 drowsy images, offering a robust support for the model to learn. The validation set (Figure 3.4) has 531 active and 509 drowsy images, whereas the testing set (Figure 3.5) has 532 and 511 images for the respective class. This equal distribution helps the model evaluation stay fair and credible, free from bias towards one class. Class balance among splits also facilitates good generalization and enables the model to generalize well on unseen instances.

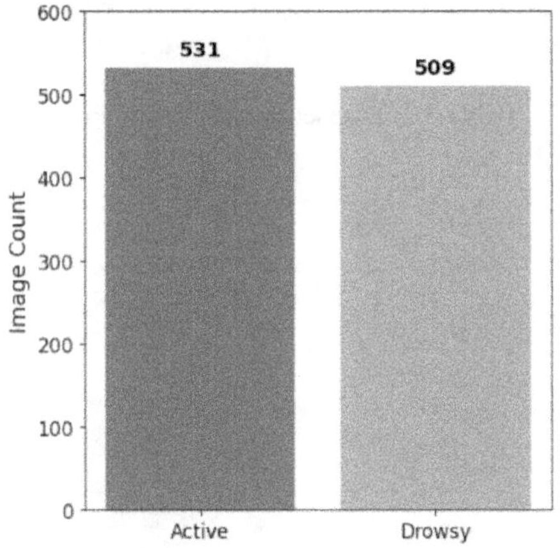

Figure 3.4. Validation set distribution

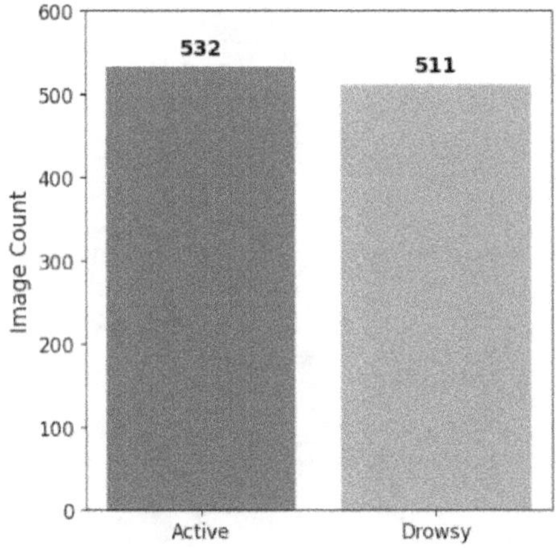

Figure 3.5. Testing set distribution

Apart from standard preprocessing, we also include a series of data augmentation strategies on the training set to artificially expand data variability and prevent overfitting. Improvements encompass rescaling, rotation, horizontal flip, scaling, width and height shift, and shearing transforms. These are performed to account for variability that can be present in real-life driving environments, such as variation in head position, lighting variations, or camera angle variations. Consequently, the model is stronger and can generalize data outside the training set. Table 3.2 provides a concise overview of the preprocessing and enhancement methods applied in this research.

Table 3.2. Dataset Preprocessing Process

Step	Description
Data Classification	Collected images were accurately classified into two separate classes, namely *active* and *sleep*, to facilitate supervised learning and direct access during model training.
Image Scaling	Each image was resized to a consistent resolution of 224 × 224 pixels using three color channels (RGB) to standardize the input size for the convolutional neural network.
Random Shuffling	Images were randomly shuffled to avoid order bias and to ensure uniform distribution of samples across training and validation subsets.
Dataset Splitting	The dataset was split into 80% training, 10% validation, and 10% testing, where the training set was used for learning, the validation set for hyperparameter tuning and overfitting control, and the testing set for unbiased performance evaluation on unseen data.
Data Augmentation	Data augmentation techniques were applied exclusively to the training subset to improve model robustness and simulate real-world driving variability.
Rescaling	Pixel values were rescaled by a factor of 1/255 to normalize them within the range [0, 1], enabling faster and more stable convergence during training.
Rotation	Images were randomly rotated within a range of ±40 degrees to allow the model to learn orientation-invariant features.
Width and Height Shift	Random shifts of up to 20% in width and height were applied to simulate off-center facial positions commonly observed in real driving scenarios.
Shear Transformation	Shear transformations of up to 20% were applied to introduce geometric distortions and improve robustness against pose variations.
Zoom	Random zooming of up to 20% was applied to make the model invariant to scale variations.
Horizontal Flipping	Images were horizontally flipped to enhance generalization across different face orientations and camera viewpoints.

3.3.3 Deep Learning Model Development and Training

The proposed research applies deep learning techniques with primary emphasis on convolutional neural networks, which became widely accepted in computer vision because they automatically learn hierarchical feature representations directly from image data without external feature engineering. CNNs are particularly appropriate for driver drowsiness detection since they capture fine facial variations, including eye closure duration and eyelid movement, which act as strong visual indicators of reduced alertness. In contrast to traditional machine learning methods, CNN-based models remove the dependency on hand-crafted feature extraction and instead learn discriminative patterns directly from raw pixel values, which improves robustness under changing illumination and imaging conditions. Visual learning in CNNs follows a hierarchical structure, where initial layers extract basic features such as edges and texture information, whereas deeper layers represent higher-level semantic characteristics related to eye state and overall facial appearance. This hierarchical representation allows CNNs to model complex visual patterns linked to drowsiness, thereby supporting real-time driver monitoring scenarios that require fast and reliable inference.

However, training CNN models from scratch is computationally expensive and typically requires large-scale annotated datasets. While shallow learning models can operate with relatively limited data, deep learning models demand substantially larger and more diverse datasets to achieve good generalization, making data collection and labeling a challenging task. In addition, CNN performance is highly dependent on proper hyperparameter tuning, including learning rate selection, optimizer configuration, and regularization strategies, which often requires multiple training iterations.

To overcome the identified limitations, this study applies a transfer learning strategy that uses pre-trained convolutional neural network architectures, which were originally trained on large-scale benchmark datasets such as ImageNet. The adopted approach does not substitute the custom eye-state dataset; instead, the pre-trained networks are fine-tuned using the prepared dataset so that previously learned generic visual features are preserved and gradually adapted to the specific task of driver drowsiness detection. This approach reduces overall training duration, improves convergence behavior, and strengthens classification accuracy, especially when the available dataset size remains moderate. A summary of the commonly used pre-trained CNN architectures examined in this study is provided in Table 3.3.

Table 3.3. Summary of Different Pre-trained Models

Model	Architectural Details	Advantages	Disadvantages	Number of Parameters
AlexNet	5 conv layers, 3 FC layers, ReLU, Max pooling, Dropout	Introduced ReLU, Dropout	Shallow, High computational cost	60 million
VGG16/19	16/19 layers, small 3x3 filters, multiple FC layers	Simple, Uniform, Easy to modify	Large parameters, High computational/memory cost	138 million (VGG16), 143 million (VGG19)
ResNet	50/101/152 layers, residual connections	Solves vanishing gradient, Enables deep networks	Complex, Increased computational cost	25.6 million (ResNet50), 44.5 million (ResNet101), 60.2 million (ResNet152)
Inception	Inception modules, multiple filter sizes, auxiliary classifiers	Efficient computation, Reduced parameters	Complex, Difficult to modify	23 million
DenseNet	Dense blocks, 121/169/201/264 layers	Efficient parameters, Improved gradient flow	Computationally intensive, Higher memory	8 million (DenseNet121), 18 million (DenseNet201)
EfficientNet	Compound scaling, variants B0 to B7	State-of-the-art performance, Efficient computation	Complex scaling, Requires tuning	5.3 million (EfficientNetB0), 19 million (EfficientNetB7)

From the comparative analysis of the evaluated convolutional neural network architectures, DenseNet121, VGG16, and EfficientNetV2B0 showed strong predictive capability in terms of classification accuracy. Even though DenseNet121 produced slightly higher accuracy values, EfficientNetV2B0 was chosen as the final model because it offered a more balanced compromise between accuracy, computational cost, and deployment practicality, which remains essential for real-time driver drowsiness detection scenarios. EfficientNetV2B0 represents a recent CNN design that applies compound scaling to jointly adjust network depth, width, and input resolution, thereby achieving improved performance without excessive parameter growth. Although it still follows a deep learning structure, EfficientNetV2B0 operates with a considerably smaller number of trainable parameters, approximately 7.8 million, when compared to heavier models such as VGG16, which leads to reduced memory usage and faster inference speed, making it more appropriate for embedded and in-vehicle systems with limited computational resources.

In this study, EfficientNetV2B0 is adopted as the base network and extended with task-specific classification layers to address the binary eye-state classification problem (active versus drowsy). These additions allow the model to learn discriminative features relevant to eye-state variations while preserving the efficiency of the base architecture. The following modifications are incorporated:

- GlobalAveragePooling2D: Global average pooling takes the spatial features of all spatial locations in the feature map and aggregates them so that the network can learn the global context instead of the fixed size of the fully connected layers.

- Dense (fully connected) layers: Additional dense layers are used to transform the pooled features into more abstract representations related to sleepiness. In other words, dense layers help the model learn more complex and subtle differences between eye states.

- Dropout layer: Dropout is a layer that reduces model overfitting by randomly turning off some neurons during training, allowing a learning penalty for the common adaptation of all input neurons. This will also improve the generalization ability of the model.

Table 3.4 details the split of the new EfficientNetV2B0 after base layers, custom additions, and classification tasks in terms of architectural details.

Table 3.4. EfficientNetV2B0 Architectural Details

Layer Type	Input Shape	Filter Size	Number of Layers	Output Shape
Input Layer	(224, 224, 3)	–	1	(224, 224, 3)
Stem Conv2D (Base)	(224, 224, 3)	3×3	1	(112, 112, 32)
MBConv1_3×3 (Base)	(112, 112, 32)	3×3	1	(112, 112, 16)
MBConv6_3×3 (Base)	(112, 112, 16)	3×3	2	(56, 56, 24)
MBConv6_5×5 (Base)	(56, 56, 24)	5×5	2	(28, 28, 40)
MBConv6_3×3 (Base)	(28, 28, 40)	3×3	3	(14, 14, 80)
MBConv6_5×5 (Base)	(14, 14, 80)	5×5	3	(7, 7, 112)
MBConv6_3×3 (Base)	(7, 7, 112)	3×3	4	(7, 7, 192)
Conv2D (Custom)	(7, 7, 192)	3×3	1	(7, 7, 128)
GlobalAveragePooling2D	(7, 7, 128)	–	1	(128)
Dense Layer	(128)	–	1	(1024)
Dropout	(1024)	–	1	(1024)
Dense Layer	(1024)	–	1	(128)
Output Layer (Dense)	(128)	–	1	(1)

To enhance the initial learning effectiveness of the selected architecture, a two-stage training procedure was applied, which included a transfer learning stage followed by a fine-tuning stage. This training scheme allows the model to first benefit from previously learned knowledge and then gradually adapt its internal representations to the specific characteristics of eye-state-based drowsiness detection. In the first stage of training, the core layers of EfficientNetV2B0 were kept frozen, and training was limited to the newly introduced classification layers only. This configuration preserves the generic visual representations acquired from ImageNet, while allowing the network to learn task-specific feature mappings related to eye-state classification. During this phase, the model was trained for 20 epochs using a learning rate of 0.001, which supported stable convergence without causing abrupt changes in the pre-trained weights. In the second stage, selected higher layers of the base network were unfrozen to allow controlled adaptation of deeper feature representations to the target dataset. For this fine-tuning stage, the learning rate was reduced to 0.0001, and training was extended for an additional 30 epochs. This gradual unfreezing combined with a lower learning rate limits overfitting and supports steady convergence behavior, especially when the available dataset size remains moderate.

3.4 PROPOSED DEEP ENSEMBLE LEARNING

In the proposed driver drowsiness detection system, a deep ensemble learning strategy is applied using two CNN models, namely a custom DenseNet121 and EfficientNetV2B0. The ensemble framework integrates the class-wise decision scores produced by DenseNet121 and EfficientNetV2B0 for both active and drowsy states. Based on these combined outputs, the framework then performs the subsequent decision-level operations.

- **Generate Confidence Scores**: Each model (DenseNet121 and EfficientNetV2B0) generates confidence scores for active and drowsy classes. Basically, these scores represent the model's confidence in predicting the respective class. From the Equ 3.1 and 3.2, Let $C_D(i)$ be the confidence score from DenseNet121 for the i-th sample and $C_E(i)$ be the confidence score from EfficientNetV2B0 for the same sample such that:

$$\mathrm{C_D}(i) = \mathrm{DenseNet121.predict}(x_i) \qquad (3.1)$$

$$\mathrm{C_E}(i) = \mathrm{EfficientNet.predict}(x_i) \qquad (3.2)$$

- **Apply Non-linear Transformations**: The prediction scores are transformed using a non-linear function (a gaussian like function) to compute uncertainty scores. These functions quantify the deviation and reward for each class based on the prediction scores. For each model the uncertainty U is computed as follows in below Equ 3.3 and 3.4:

$$\mathrm{U_D}(i) = 1 - exp\left(-\frac{(\mathrm{C_D}(i)-1)^2}{2}\right) \qquad (3.3)$$

$$\mathrm{U_E}(i) = 1 - exp\left(-\frac{(\mathrm{C_E}(i)-1)^2}{2}\right) \qquad (3.4)$$

- **Calculate confidence Values**: The rank values for each class are computed as the product of the confidence scores from the non-linear function as mentioned in Equ 3.5

and 3.6. This combines the confidence scores with the uncertainty values to form a weighted confidence measure.

$$\mathrm{R_D}(i) = \mathrm{U_D}(i) \times \mathrm{C_D}(i) \tag{3.5}$$

$$\mathrm{R_E}(i) = \mathrm{U_E}(i) \times \mathrm{C_E}(i) \tag{3.6}$$

- **Compute Average confidence and Aggregate Values**: The rank values from both models are aggregated to form a combined score for each class as mentioned in Equ 3.7. This can be done by averaging the rank values.

$$R_{avg}(i) = \frac{R_D(i)+R_E(i)}{2} \tag{3.7}$$

- **Determine Final Classification**: Finally, using Equ 3.8, we combine the uncertainties with the confidence scores to form the final score, which is then used to determine the classification. This final score represents the average contribution of the two models, jointly accounting for their confidence and uncertainty estimates, and is numerically expressed as follows:

$$\text{Final\_score }(i) = \frac{U_D(i)\times R_{avg}(i)+\mathrm{U}_E(i)\times R_{avg}(i)}{2} \tag{3.8}$$

From Equation 3.9, the final class decision depends on a predefined threshold value. When the computed score exceeds 0.5, the input is classified as “drowsy”; however, if the score remains equal to or below this threshold, the predicted class is “active”.

$$Prediction(i) = \begin{cases} 1 & if\ final\ score(i) > 0.5 \\ 0 & otherwise \end{cases} \tag{3.9}$$

Finally, the ensemble model accuracy is calculated by comparing the predicted class outputs with the corresponding ground-truth labels, as defined in Equation 3.10 below.

$$\text{Accuracy} = \frac{\Sigma(\text{predictions==lables})}{\text{len(lables)}} \tag{3.10}$$

3.5 RESULTS AND DISCUSSION

The proposed driver drowsiness detection system was designed and implemented using the Python programming language, with development carried out through the Anaconda distribution on a Windows 10 platform. This section reports and analyzes the experimental results obtained from model evaluation by applying standard performance metrics, namely accuracy, precision, recall, and F1-score, which are discussed in detail in the following subsections.

$$P = \frac{TP}{(TP+FP)} \qquad (3.11)$$

From Equ 3.11, P denotes the precision metric, which quantifies the proportion of positive predictions corresponding to the (active driver) class that are correctly identified. Here, TP represents true positives, where the driver is (correctly classified as active), and FP denotes false positives, where the driver is (incorrectly classified as active).

$$\mathrm{R} = \frac{TP}{(\mathrm{TP+FN})} \qquad (3.12)$$

From Equ 3.12, R represents the recall metric, which evaluates the proportion of actual positive cases, that is, (drivers who were active), that were correctly detected by the model. In this expression, FN denotes false negatives, where an active driver is (incorrectly classified as drowsy). This measure is also known as sensitivity and is particularly important in situations where the impact of false-negative decisions is high.

$$\mathrm{F1} = 2 \times \frac{R \times P}{\mathrm{R}+P} \qquad (3.13)$$

From Equ 3.13, F1 denotes the F1-score, which is computed as the harmonic mean of precision P and recall R. This metric provides a balanced performance measure, particularly in scenarios where the class distribution is uneven.

Figure 3.6 compares and analyzes several CNN models such as AlexNet, VGG16, ResNet50, InceptionV3, DenseNet121, and EfficientNetV2B0. These models share the same dataset and hyperparameters in the same environment and provide fair performance comparison of various models. The comparative analysis primarily relied on classification accuracy to evaluate the ability of each model to distinguish between active and sleepy eye states. Among the evaluated architectures, DenseNet121 and EfficientNetV2B0 achieved the highest accuracy of 91%, followed closely by VGG16, which recorded an accuracy of 90%.

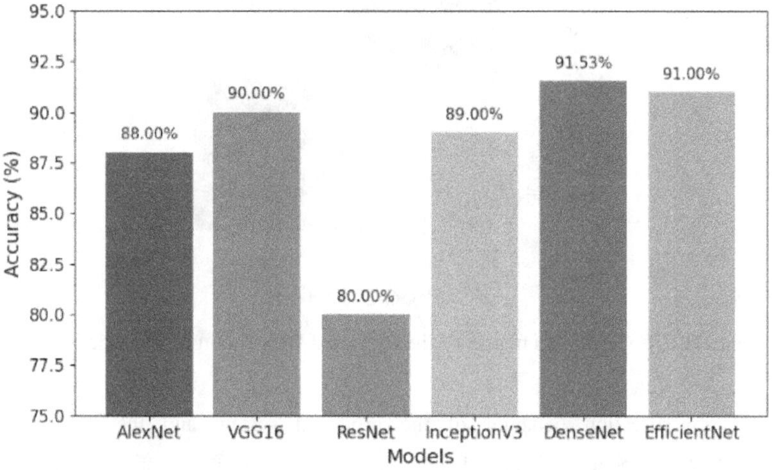

Figure 3.6. Comparative Analysis for different model

The obtained results suggest that deep network architectures with appropriate structural tuning generally yield improved performance for binary eye-state classification. Although InceptionV3 produced a marginally lower accuracy of 89%, it still performed better than AlexNet, which achieved 88%, and ResNet50, which reported the lowest accuracy of 80%. Even with a relatively large custom dataset exceeding 10,000 images, ResNet50 showed sensitivity to overfitting because of its depth and high parameter complexity, which reduced its suitability for this task. VGG16 delivered competitive accuracy; however, its large parameter size and higher memory demand restrict its applicability in real-time environments with limited computational resources. In a similar manner, InceptionV3 effectively captures multi-scale visual features, but its complex architecture leads to increased inference time, which can negatively impact real-time operation. Consequently, EfficientNetV2B0 was chosen as the primary model for fine-tuning due to its balanced performance in terms of accuracy and computational efficiency, whereas DenseNet121 was retained within the ensemble framework to improve robustness and generalization capability. Therefore, the final model selection is guided not only by accuracy values, but also by considerations related to architectural efficiency, scalability, and deployment feasibility, which remain essential for practical intelligent transportation system applications.

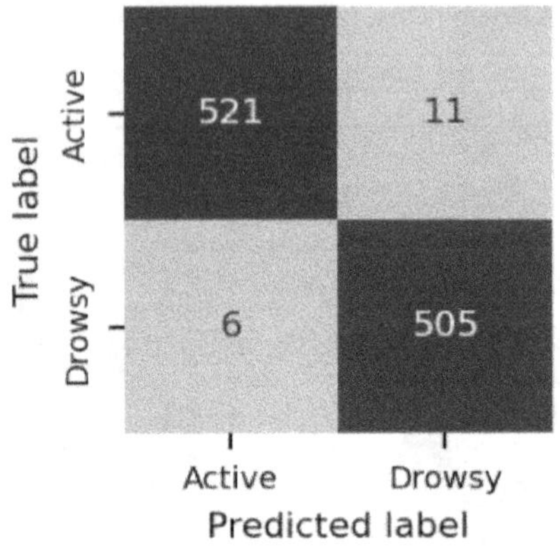

Figure 3.7. Confusion matrix of the proposed DL (Fine-tuned EfficientNet)

The classification behavior of the proposed system and the final fine-tuned EfficientNetV2B0 model is illustrated through the confusion matrix obtained from the test dataset, as shown in Figure 3.7. The confusion matrix indicates that the model correctly identified 521 images as active and 505 images as sleepy, corresponding to true positive and true negative predictions, respectively. In contrast, 11 active samples were incorrectly predicted as sleepy, representing false negatives, and 6 sleepy samples were wrongly classified as active, representing false positives. The limited number of incorrect predictions reflects the model's ability to distinguish between the two eye-state classes with high reliability. Overall, the confusion matrix results support the accuracy and dependable performance of the EfficientNetV2B0 model for driver drowsiness detection.

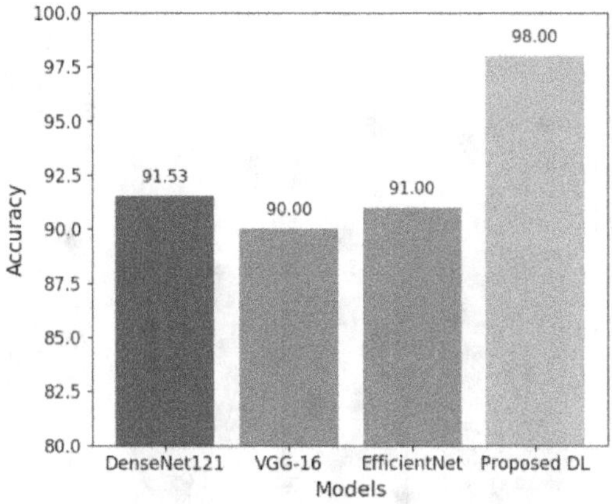

Figure 3.8. Comparative analysis in terms of accuracy

Figure 3.8 presents a comparative visual analysis of the fine-tuned EfficientNet model against selected baseline CNN architectures that were previously implemented in this study, namely DenseNet121, VGG16, and the base version of EfficientNetV2B0. The comparison relies on the final classification accuracy values, where each model was trained using the same dataset and evaluated under identical experimental conditions. Among the baseline architectures, DenseNet121 achieved the highest accuracy of 91.53%, followed by EfficientNetV2B0 with an accuracy of 91.00%, whereas VGG16 recorded an accuracy of 90.00%. The proposed model, which we refer to as fine-tuned EfficientNetV2B0 with added custom layers and an improved training regime, produced consistently better results across every dataset assessed. For example, the proposed model achieved 98.00% accuracy, which is a significant improvement (over 6.5%) than the next best performing baseline model (DenseNet121). The results clearly provided improvement and consistently show marked improvement for all metrics, which demonstrates the depth of the proposed deep learning model and framework.

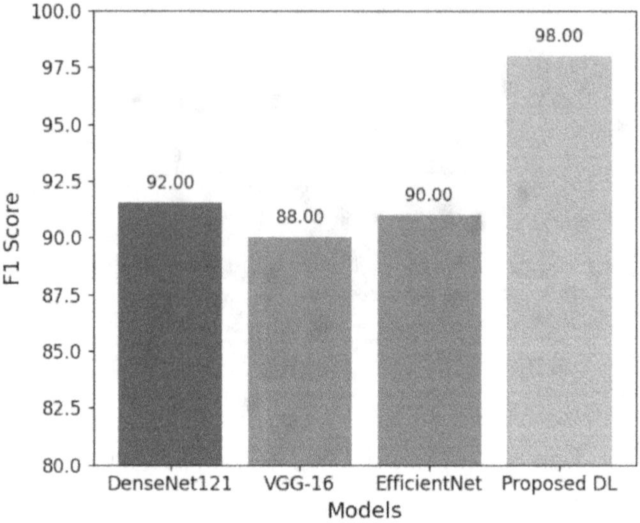

Figure 3.9. Comparative analysis in terms of F1-score

Figure 3.9 illustrates the comparison of F1-score values obtained from the best-performing CNN architectures, including DenseNet121, VGG16, EfficientNetV2B0, and the proposed fine-tuned EfficientNet model. As the F1-score represents the harmonic mean of precision and recall, it offers a more comprehensive evaluation of model performance, particularly under conditions of class imbalance or when false-positive and false-negative errors have comparable impact. The F1 score of DenseNet121 reaches 92.00, but the overall balance of sensitivity and specificity is still surprisingly good. EfficientNetV2B0 achieves the second best F1 score of 90.00, while VGG16 is only slightly behind at 88.00. Our proposed and fine-tuned model adopts a unique training strategy to train an additional classification layer and achieve a higher F1 score of 98.00. The increase in F1 score shows the success of the overall feature extraction, classification, and training strategy.

Figure 3.10 presents the confusion matrix for the proposed ensemble learning model, which combines DenseNet121 and EfficientNetV2B0. The matrix highlights the model's strong classification ability, correctly identifying 527 out of 532 active instances and 500 out of 511 drowsy instances. Only a small number of samples were misclassified 5 actives labeled as drowsy and 11 drowsy labeled as active. This low error rate reflects the ensemble's high precision and recalls for both classes.

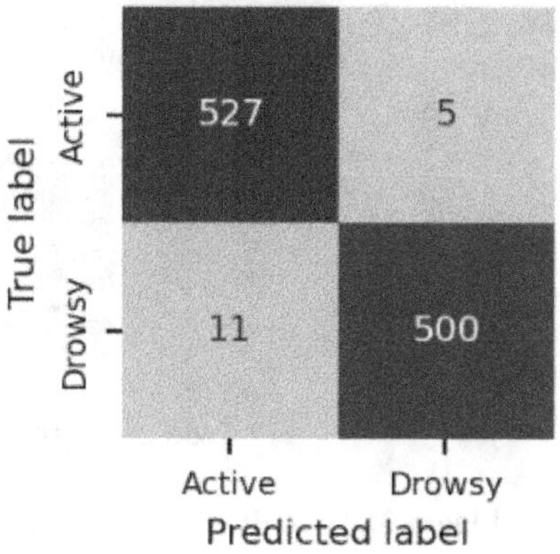

Figure 3.10. Confusion matrix

Table 3.5 represents the proposed ensemble model that achieved the highest accuracy of 99%. Both precision and recall for the Active and Drowsy classes are extremely high, approaching or reaching 0.99. The outcome validates the effectiveness of the ensemble strategy towards capturing complex variations in eye states under diverse conditions and the near-perfect metrics confirm the model's suitability for deployment in real-time driver monitoring systems.

Table 3.5. Class wise quantified outcome

Class	**Precision**	**Recall**	**F1-score**	**Samples**
Active	0.98	0.99	0.99	532
Drowsy	0.99	0.98	0.98	511
Accuracy	0.99			

To conduct benchmarking of the proposed approach, this study considered a widely used public dataset, namely the MRL Eye dataset, which contains static eye images captured under different lighting conditions (MRL, 2025). Figure 3.11 shows the confusion matrix obtained for the DenseNet121 model when evaluated on the MRL Eye dataset, providing insight into its classification behavior under standardized benchmarking conditions.

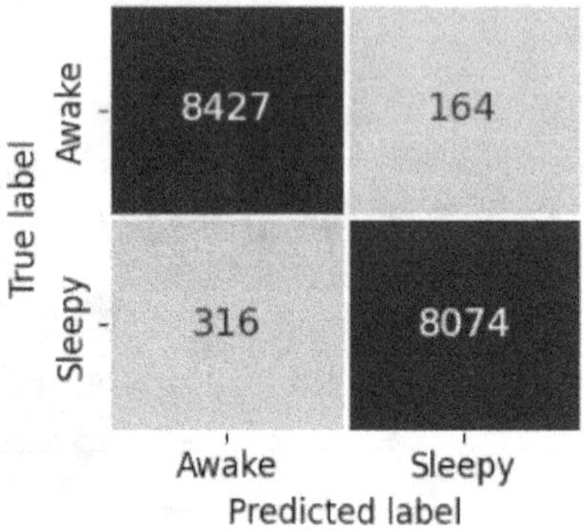

Figure 3.11. Confusion matrix DenseNet

The model correctly classified 8427 awake and 8074 sleepy instances. It misclassified 164 awake images as sleepy (false positives) and 316 sleepy images as awake (false negatives). These results reflect a high classification performance, with the majority of samples correctly identified. However, the higher number of false negatives indicates a slight bias toward predicting the awake class, which may be critical in safety-sensitive applications like driver drowsiness detection.

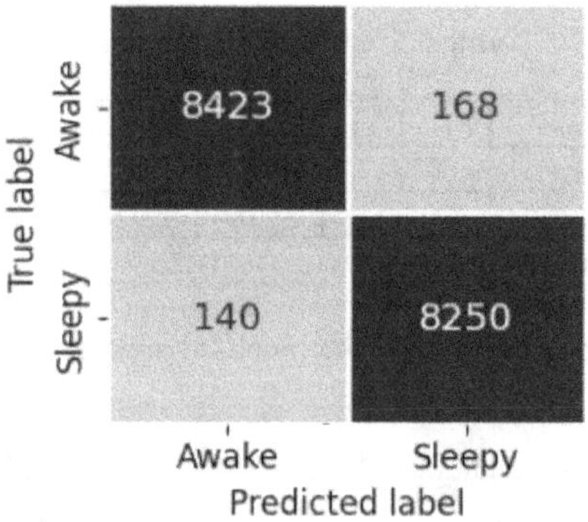

Figure 3.12. Confusion matrix EfficientNet

Figure 3.12 shows the confusion matrix for the EfficientNetV2B0 model tested on the MRL Eye dataset. The model correctly classified 8423 awake and 8250 sleepy instances. It misclassified 168 awake images as sleepy (false positives) and only 140 sleepy images as awake (false negatives). When compared to DenseNet121, EfficientNetV2B0 achieved fewer false negatives, which is particularly important in drowsiness detection scenarios were failing to identify a sleepy driver poses greater risk. Overall, the model demonstrates excellent balance between both classes, contributing to its high precision and recall.

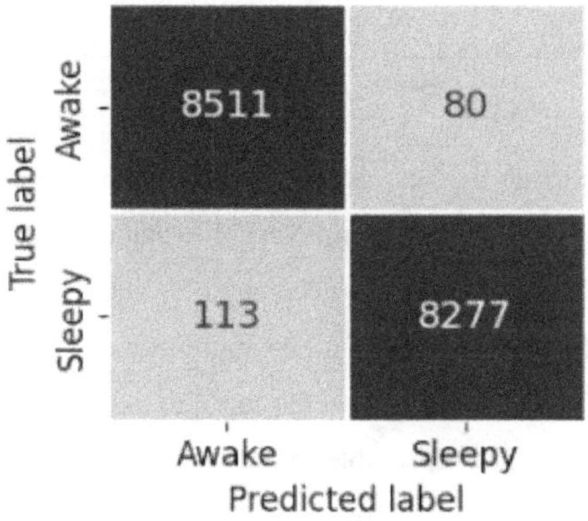

Figure 3.13. Confusion matrix Ensemble

Figure 3.13 presents the confusion matrix corresponding to the ensemble model formed by combining DenseNet121 and EfficientNetV2B0. The ensemble correctly classified 8511 instances as awake and 8277 instances as sleepy, reflecting a high level of prediction accuracy across both classes. Only 80 awake samples were incorrectly predicted as sleepy, representing false positives, and 113 sleepy samples were misclassified as awake, representing false negatives. These misclassification counts are the lowest among all the evaluated models, which highlights the improved effectiveness of the ensemble strategy. The large proportion of correct predictions for both eye states confirms that the ensemble model captures complex visual characteristics more reliably, making it suitable for deployment in real-time driver drowsiness detection applications.

Table 3.6. Shows class-wise performance on MRL Eye Dataset

Model	Class	Precision	Recall	F1-Score	Accuracy
DenseNet121	Awake	0.96	0.98	0.97	97.00%
	Sleepy	0.98	0.96	0.97	
EfficientNetV2B0	Awake	0.98	0.98	0.98	98.00%
	Sleepy	0.98	0.98	0.98	
Ensemble Model	Awake	0.99	0.99	0.99	99.00%
	Sleepy	0.99	0.99	0.99	

Table 3.6 summarizes the class-wise performance comparison obtained on the MRL Eye dataset. The results show that DenseNet121 provided balanced performance across both eye-state classes, achieving an overall accuracy of 97.00% with slightly higher precision for the sleepy class. EfficientNetV2B0 further strengthened prediction results by reaching an accuracy of 98.00% and maintaining consistent precision and recall values for both awake and sleepy categories. The ensemble model surpassed the individual architectures by combining complementary feature representations learned by DenseNet121 and EfficientNetV2B0, which helped reduce model-specific bias and correct individual misclassification behavior. Consequently, the ensemble achieved the highest accuracy of 99.00%, along with near-perfect precision, recall, and F1-score values of 0.99 for both classes. These results confirm that integrating predictions from structurally diverse CNN models improves robustness and minimizes false-positive and false-negative errors, which is especially important for safety-critical driver drowsiness detection systems.

Table 3.6 provides a comparative evaluation of the proposed ensemble model against existing literature on driver drowsiness detection. Prior studies, such as Zhang et al. (2018) and Li & Lee (2019), employed conventional CNN or hybrid feature-based models, achieving accuracy scores around 88–91%. Although Kim et al. (2020) and Patel et al. (2021) improved performance using deeper networks like ResNet-50 and MobileNetV2, their results were still constrained by limited dataset diversity and model capacity.

Table 3.7. Comparative Analysis on the MRL dataset

Study	Method/Model	Accuracy
Kongcharoen et al. (2020)	Haar cascade + CNN	94%
Suresh et al. (2021)	CNN	86.05%
Walizad et al. (2022)	CNN	95%
Tibrewal et al. (2021)	TEDD + CNN	95%
Jahan et al. (2023)	4D model	97.53%
Makhmudov et al. (2024)	VGG16; CNN	95.85%; 96.54%
Salem & Waleed (2024)	CNN; MobileNetV2	96%, 97%
Proposed	Ensemble (DenseNet121 & EfficientNetB0)	99%

Table 3.7 provides a comparative analysis between the proposed ensemble model and previously reported driver drowsiness detection approaches available in the literature. The surveyed studies follow varied methodological directions, where some methods combine Haar cascade–based eye or face detection with CNN classifiers, in which handcrafted Haar-like features support fast object localization prior to deep learning–based classification (Kongcharoen et al., 2020). Other works rely on standalone CNN architectures that directly learn discriminative visual features from raw image inputs. Moreover, hybrid frameworks such as TEDD + CNN and 4D-based models were introduced, where TEDD models temporal eye behaviors including blink duration and closure patterns, and 4D approaches jointly utilize spatial facial characteristics and temporal dependencies across successive frames (Tibrewal et al., 2021; Jahan et al., 2023). Reported classification accuracies across these methods range from 86.05% (Suresh et al., 2021) to 97.53% (Jahan et al., 2023). More recent deep learning architectures such as VGG16 and MobileNetV2 achieved accuracy values between 95.85% and 97% (Makhmudov et al., 2024; Salem and Waleed, 2024). In comparison, the proposed ensemble framework, which integrates DenseNet121 and EfficientNetB0, attains an accuracy of 99% on the MRL Eye dataset by combining complementary feature representations and limiting individual model misclassification tendencies. These results demonstrate that ensemble-based learning improves robustness and reliability, which is essential for real-time driver drowsiness detection applications.

Beyond classification accuracy, the proposed ensemble framework was developed with careful consideration of computational efficiency and practical deployment within automotive environments. In deep learning systems, computational load is strongly influenced by the number of trainable parameters and related floating-point operations, which directly affect memory usage, inference delay, and power consumption. In this study, EfficientNetV2B0 and DenseNet121 were intentionally chosen to maintain a balance between prediction accuracy and parameter efficiency. EfficientNetV2B0 contains approximately 7 million trainable parameters, whereas DenseNet121 includes nearly 8 million parameters, both of which remain considerably lower than conventional deep architectures such as VGG16 with around 138 million parameters and deeper ResNet variants such as ResNet152 with nearly 60 million parameters. Despite their relatively compact structure, EfficientNetV2B0 applies compound scaling to jointly regulate network depth, width, and input resolution, whereas DenseNet121 benefits from dense feature reuse that minimizes redundant computation and supports effective gradient propagation. All experimental evaluations were performed on CPU-based systems to realistically represent in-vehicle, edge, or embedded deployment conditions, where high-performance GPUs may not be available. This implementation choice supports the broader objective of the thesis to develop scalable, cost-efficient, and real-time driver monitoring solutions suitable for resource-limited automotive platforms.

3.6 SUMMARY

This chapter described a deep learning–based ensemble framework for driver drowsiness detection using eye-state information extracted from facial images. The main goal was to design a robust and computationally efficient eye-based detection system through a systematic evaluation of multiple convolutional neural network architectures. For this purpose, several commonly adopted CNN models were implemented, among which DenseNet121 and EfficientNetV2B0 showed superior performance in terms of classification accuracy and generalization behavior. Experimental evaluation indicated that DenseNet121 and EfficientNetV2B0 achieved accuracy values of 97% and 98%, respectively. The observed performance improvement can be attributed to their complementary architectural characteristics, where DenseNet121 supports effective feature reuse through dense connectivity, and EfficientNetV2B0 provides a balanced trade-off between accuracy and parameter efficiency using compound scaling. Based on these findings, an ensemble learning strategy was applied to integrate both architectures. The resulting ensemble model achieved an accuracy of 99%, which confirms that combining heterogeneous feature representations reduces individual model bias and enhances robustness against subtle eye-state variations caused by illumination changes, facial accessories, or partial eye closure. This fusion process produces more stable and reliable predictions when compared to single-model approaches. Overall, the proposed framework maintains an effective balance between detection performance and computational efficiency, which supports its suitability for real-time driver monitoring systems. However, the current implementation focuses on static eye-state analysis and does not consider additional behavioral or temporal indicators such as yawning patterns or blink dynamics. These limitations are addressed in Chapters 4 and 5, where the framework is extended toward real-time video-based analysis and multi-feature drowsiness detection.

CHAPTER-4

HYBRID AI FRAMEWORK FOR DRIVER DROWSINESS DETECTION BASED ON BEHAVIORAL CUES FROM FACIAL INDICATORS IN LIVE CONDITIONS

4.1 INTRODUCTION

The growing number of safety concerns on road networks has strengthened research activity within Intelligent Transportation Systems, where driver drowsiness detection remains a critical safety-oriented application. This chapter presents a real-time hybrid AI framework that combines deep learning and machine learning techniques to analyze facial behavioral cues for detecting driver drowsiness under live driving conditions. The proposed system operates on visual input captured through a monocular camera and concentrates on extracting reliable facial indicators such as eye closure and yawning patterns. In contrast to conventional webcam-based solutions reported in earlier studies, which often suffered performance degradation under low illumination and varying lighting environments, the proposed framework addresses these challenges through robust facial landmark modeling and feature normalization strategies, allowing consistent operation across diverse environmental conditions. In addition, this chapter introduces a lightweight facial landmark detection module based on a support vector machine classifier. The selection of SVM is driven by its low computational overhead and its established effectiveness in handling regression and classification tasks on low-dimensional geometric facial features, especially under limited training data and strict real-time constraints. By separating landmark localization from deep feature learning, the proposed framework preserves high detection accuracy and ensures low-latency execution, which is essential for real-time in-vehicle deployment.

4.2 PROBLEM DESCRIPTION

Driver drowsiness detection research generally followed two dominant directions, namely i) deep learning–based image classification and ii) classical geometric analysis using facial landmarks. Deep learning approaches, particularly CNN-based models, achieved high accuracy when classifying drowsy and alert driver states from facial images. These models learn complex visual representations from large-scale datasets and detect subtle fatigue-related cues such as prolonged eye closure or yawning patterns. However, CNN-based classifiers also remain susceptible to false predictions, where a drowsy driver may not be detected correctly due to uncertainty introduced by real-world driving conditions. Such conditions include illumination variation, partial facial occlusion caused by accessories such as caps, and changes in facial pose during driving. In binary classification problems such as driver drowsiness detection, deep learning models commonly use a sigmoid activation function in the final output layer. The sigmoid function (Goodfellow et al., 2016) converts the raw network output into a probability value within the range of 0 to 1, which represents the likelihood that the input sample belongs to the positive class, defined here as the *drowsy* state, and it can be mathematically expressed as follows:

$$\mathrm{P(drowsy)} = \sigma(z) = \frac{1}{1+\mathrm{e}^{-\mathrm{z}}} \tag{4.1}$$

Equation (4.1) represents the sigmoid function, where *z* denotes the raw output of the network before activation, commonly referred to as the logit, which reflects the unnormalized confidence produced by the model. The prediction is classified as *drowsy* if the resulting probability exceeds a predefined threshold (commonly 0.5), and as *non-drowsy* otherwise. Though the sigmoid function yields a discrete class label, it also assigns a probabilistic confidence score to each class, enabling interpretation of prediction reliability. One major concern with deep learning models is the uncertainty in classification confidence. For example, suppose a model receives an input image of a drowsy driver and provided output logits $z = 0.2$ then $\mathrm{P(drowsy)}$ can be computed as follows:

$$\mathrm{P(drowsy)} = \frac{1}{1+\mathrm{e}^{-0.2}} \approx 0.55 \tag{4.2}$$

The above Equ 4.2 shows that the model has predicted image as drowsy with 55% confidence, and by complementarity the non-drowsiness class shows 45% of confidence score such that from Equ 4.3 as follows:

$$\mathrm{P}\left(\mathrm{non}_{\mathrm{drowsy}}\right) = 1 - \mathrm{P(drowsy)} = 0.45 \tag{4.3}$$

Although the model labels the input as 'drowsy' (since 0.55 > 0.45), the small margin between the two probabilities indicates low confidence shown in Figure 4.1.

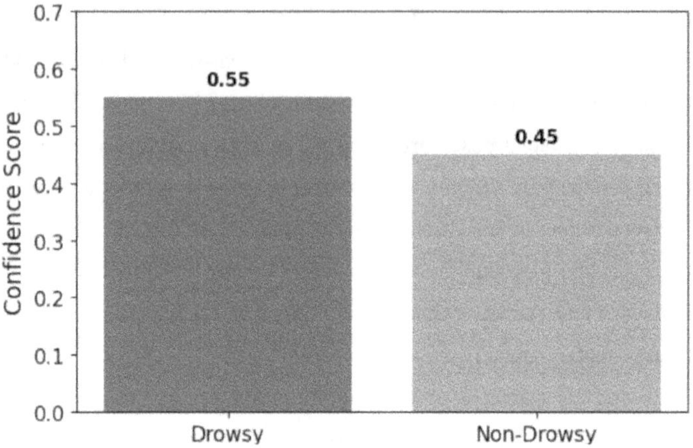

Figure 4.1. Illustrative scenario of uncertainty in classification confidence by DL model

Based on Figure 4.1 the model technically classifies the image as drowsy, but the narrow margin indicates low confidence in its decision and in safety-critical applications like driver monitoring, such uncertainty can lead to unreliable alerts, false alarms, or missed detections. Therefore, relying solely on CNN predictions without accounting for confidence scores or integrating additional behavioral cues can compromise system reliability, especially in real-time, dynamic driving environments.

Existing research reports several lightweight driver drowsiness detection systems that depend on behavioral cues derived from geometric facial measurements, such as Eye Aspect Ratio and Mouth Aspect Ratio, which are calculated using facial landmarks obtained from pre-trained detectors including the dlib 68-point landmark model (Kazemi and Sullivan, 2014). These geometry-driven methods offer low computational overhead and support real-time execution; however, they often suffer from limited generalization and increased sensitivity to inaccuracies in landmark localization. The landmark detector provided by dlib assumes near-frontal facial orientation, which leads to unstable or imprecise landmark estimation when natural head movements occur, such as downward gaze, sideward head rotation, or partial facial occlusion. Such pose variations are common during real driving conditions and frequently result in unreliable EAR and MAR values, which in turn reduce detection reliability. Moreover, many existing studies handle geometric indicators and CNN-based predictions as separate decision modules, without applying an adaptive or confidence-aware fusion mechanism, which limits the system's ability to handle ambiguous inputs or low-confidence prediction scenarios effectively.

Despite the extensive literature on both landmark-based and deep learning–based approaches, there remains a clear lack of integrated frameworks that systematically combine the computational efficiency of geometric methods with the representational robustness of deep learning models, a gap that is directly addressed within the scope of this thesis. Existing studies predominantly rely on either lightweight landmark-based indicators or deep learning classifiers in isolation, without a coordinated multi-stage decision fusion strategy capable of reliable operation under real-world driving conditions. Furthermore, most reported systems do not incorporate adaptive mechanisms that enable the complementary use of global visual representations learned by CNN models and local geometric cues such as EAR and MAR, particularly in the presence of head pose variations, illumination changes, or partial occlusions. The proposed research progressively addresses these limitations by establishing a robust eye-state learning model and extending it into an integrated real-time framework that combines deep learning–based feature representation with lightweight machine learning–driven landmark analysis and adaptive threshold-based decision logic, followed by higher-level multi-feature reasoning to enhance detection reliability.

- **Lack of Lightweight Alternatives:** No suitable replacement for Dlib-based facial landmark detection that maintains real-time performance and pose robustness.

- **Absence of Multi-modal Fusion:** Behavioral cues (EAR, MAR) and learned CNN features are often used in isolation, without intelligent integration for improved prediction accuracy.

- **No Adaptive Decision-Making:** Current systems lack mechanisms to dynamically verify eye states by cross-referencing both EAR and CNN outputs for enhanced confidence.

- **Inadequate Thresholding & Temporal Logic:** Few studies incorporate optimal threshold tuning or frame-based persistence logic to minimize false positives/negatives in continuous video streams.

The proposed research work in this chapter addresses the above-mentioned problem by introducing a lightweight facial landmark detection module based on SVM, optimized for real-time inference, and integrating it with a pre-trained deep learning model through a multi-stage decision fusion framework. The next section discusses the proposed computational framework design.

4.3 PROPOSED FRAMEWORK DESIGN

The implementation of the system focuses on designing an integrated machine and deep learning scheme to reliably identify indicative facial landmarks for predictive LoV state or drowsiness. Figure 4.2 shows the schematic architecture and workflow process of the proposed system.

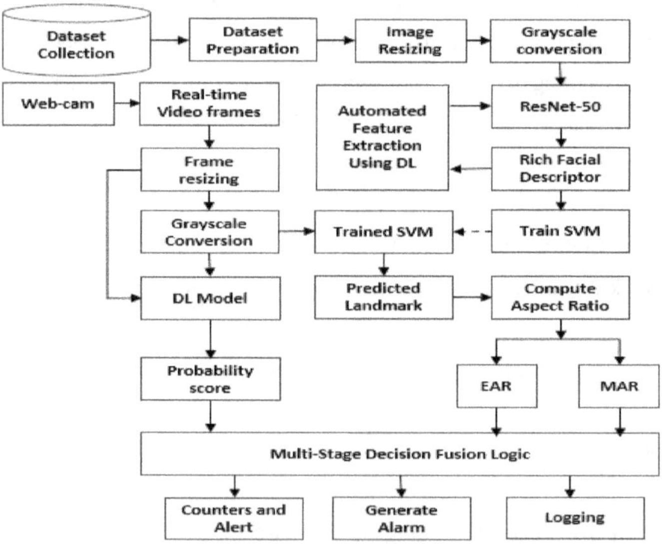

Figure 4.2. Illustration of Framework design and methodology workflow

The complete modeling of the proposed system follows three major implementation phases. In the first phase, facial landmark prediction is performed using a supervised machine learning classifier, where an offline dataset preparation step is initially carried out, followed by automated facial feature extraction through a pre-trained ResNet-50 convolutional neural network, and subsequent training of an SVM classifier. This trained SVM model is later applied during real-time operation to estimate facial landmark positions from incoming video frames. The second phase focuses on behavioral cue computation from facial imagery, where Eye Aspect Ratio and Mouth Aspect Ratio values are derived using the landmarks predicted by the SVM model, and simultaneously a deep learning–based eye-state classification network generates a probability score that indicates the likelihood of drowsiness based on eye condition. In the final phase, a multi-level decision fusion mechanism combines EAR, MAR, and CNN-derived probability scores through predefined threshold rules and temporal counters to reliably identify drowsiness or yawning events, activate alert notifications, and record detected events for subsequent analysis. The structural design and functional workflow of each module are discussed in detail in the following sections.

4.3.1 Facial Landmark Prediction

The proposed facial landmark detection methodology adopts a hybrid strategy that integrates deep learning with classical machine learning techniques. This approach uses a pre-trained CNN model to extract discriminative deep visual features from facial images, followed by a support vector machine model that performs facial landmark prediction through regression learning. The overall design focuses on learning essential image representations using deep feature extraction and then applying machine learning–based regression to accurately estimate landmark locations under real-time operating constraints.

4.3.1.1 Dataset Preparation

The initial operation in this implementation phase involves dataset preparation, as depicted in Figure 4.3. The adopted data preparation process is structured into three distinct stages, identified as Stage-A, Stage-B, and Stage-C, where each stage performs a specific role in constructing the landmark training dataset. In Stage-A, referred to as public dataset aggregation, several publicly available facial landmark datasets, including Annotated Faces in-the-Wild (AFW) (Köstinger et al., 2011), Helen, and Labeled Face Parts in-the-Wild

(LFPW), are collected and combined to form an initial labeled dataset containing facial images along with their annotated landmark coordinates. Alongside this, a custom dataset is also created by collecting facial images from online sources to introduce additional variability in pose, illumination conditions, and facial appearance. In Stage-B, which focuses on landmark generation for the custom data, the collected images are processed using the Dlib-68 facial landmark predictor to automatically generate landmark annotations that act as ground-truth labels for the custom samples. This step maintains consistency between manually annotated public datasets and automatically generated landmark representations. In Stage-C, all datasets obtained from Stage-A and Stage-B are merged to produce a unified and comprehensive dataset, which is organized into structured directories containing facial images and their corresponding landmark coordinate files. This consolidated dataset is subsequently used to train the supervised facial landmark prediction model.

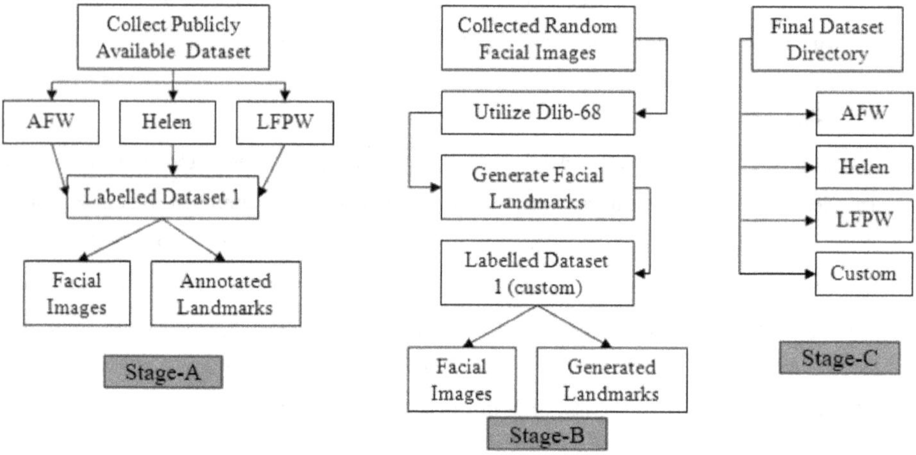

Figure 4.3. Shows the schematic outline of the data preparation strategy.

4.3.1.2 Dlib

Dlib-68 refers to a pre-trained machine learning model provided through the open-source Dlib toolkit, which offers several well-established implementations for computer vision and machine learning tasks. In facial analysis applications, Dlib is widely recognized for its 68-point facial landmark detector that is built using an ensemble of regression trees. This model was frequently applied in real-time systems because it offers a practical balance between detection speed and localization accuracy under moderate computational constraints.

Within the proposed framework, Dlib is applied during the dataset preparation stage to generate ground-truth facial landmark annotations required for training the supervised learning model. For each input facial image, the Dlib landmark predictor estimates 68 predefined landmark locations that correspond to prominent facial regions such as the eyes, eyebrows, nose, mouth, and jawline. Each landmark is represented by an (x, y) coordinate pair, which results in a total of 136 numerical values per image. The landmark predictor was trained on a large collection of facial images to reliably identify these key facial structures under varied conditions. As illustrated in Figure 4.4, the 68 landmark points are distributed across critical facial areas, clearly outlining the geometric structure of the face through points located around the eyes, eyebrows, nose, mouth, and jawline.

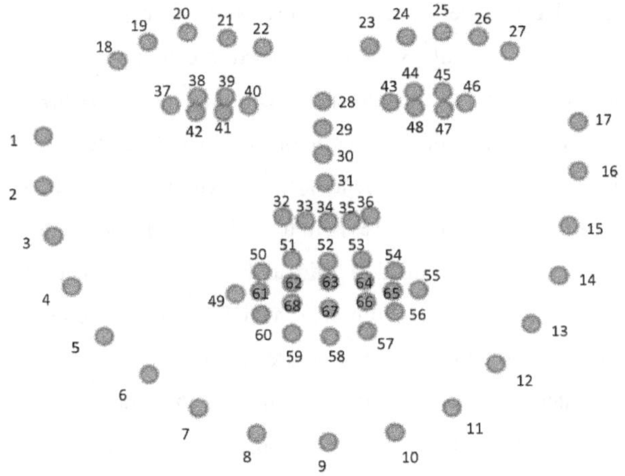

Figure 4.4. Face landmark representation (Kumari et al., 2021)

The facial landmark detection model applies Histogram of Oriented Gradients (HOG) features together with an ensemble of regression trees to estimate the spatial locations of facial landmarks. HOG represents a commonly used hand-crafted feature descriptor in computer vision that encodes local shape and appearance by capturing the distribution of edge orientations, which makes it well suited for structured objects such as human faces. In this method, HOG features are derived by computing image gradients and encoding their magnitude and orientation within localized regions, thereby emphasizing edge and contour patterns and maintaining relative robustness against illumination variation. The facial image is first divided into small spatial units known as cells, and for each cell a histogram of gradient directions is calculated. These histograms are then normalized across larger regions, referred to as blocks, in order to improve stability against contrast changes. The resulting HOG feature vectors are provided as input to the ensemble of regression trees, which progressively refine landmark locations by learning the spatial dependencies among facial components. This combined strategy supports efficient and reliable landmark localization by relying on gradient-based facial geometry instead of raw pixel intensities, which is important for real-time operation under moderate pose and lighting changes.

$$HOG = \{H_1, H_2, \cdots, H_n\} \tag{4.4}$$

From Equation 4.4, H_i denotes the histogram of gradient orientations calculated within the i-th spatial cell, where each cell corresponds to a small fixed-size rectangular region of the facial image, typically 8 × 8 pixels, used to capture localized edge and contour characteristics. Segmenting the image into such localized cells allows the HOG descriptor to preserve the spatial arrangement of facial components, including the eyes, nose, and mouth, which is essential for accurate facial landmark estimation. Using these extracted HOG features as input, an ensemble of regression trees is applied to predict facial landmark positions. Each regression tree is trained to estimate landmark coordinates based on gradient-driven facial representations learned from annotated facial images containing ground-truth landmark locations. Within the ensemble structure, successive trees focus on correcting the residual errors generated by preceding trees, which leads to gradual refinement of landmark predictions. The final estimated landmark position $\hat{L}$ (Zhao et al., 2016) is expressed by Equation 4.5 as given below.

$$\hat{L} = \sum_{i=1}^{N} T_i(HOG) \tag{4.5}$$

where T_i denotes the i-th regression tree within the ensemble and NNN represents the total number of trees used in the model. Each regression tree T_i receives the extracted HOG feature vector as input and produces an estimated landmark position as output (Yuan, Lin and Meng, 2018). During training, the model refines landmark predictions by minimizing the

Euclidean distance between the predicted landmark coordinates and the corresponding ground-truth positions, which guides the ensemble toward accurate spatial localization of facial landmarks.

$$\text{Loss} = \sum_{i=1}^{M} \left| L_i - \hat{L} \right|^2 \qquad (4.6)$$

In Equ 4.6, M is the number of landmarks, L_i is the true position and $\hat{L}$ is the predicted position.

4.3.1.3 Development and Testing Dataset

In order to train and evaluate the facial landmark detection model, this study adopts a structured dataset preparation pipeline that supports both deep feature extraction and supervised machine learning–based regression. The objective is to expose the model to a sufficiently diverse and representative set of facial images captured under varying pose, illumination, and appearance conditions. Figure 4.5 illustrates the complete workflow used for constructing the training, validation, and testing datasets.

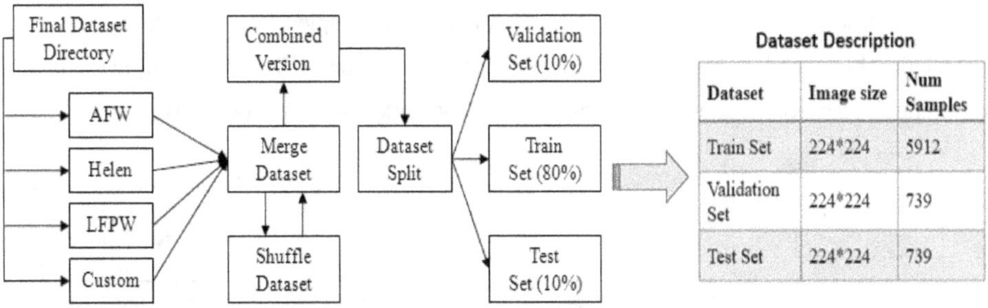

Figure 4.5. Procedure adopted in development and testing dataset preparation

As illustrated in Figure 4.5, facial image samples obtained from Annotated Faces in the Wild (AFW), Helen, Labeled Face Parts in the Wild (LFPW), and the custom-collected dataset are initially combined to form a single unified dataset, where each dataset is explicitly referenced to avoid ambiguity caused by acronym usage within the workflow. The unified dataset is then randomly shuffled to remove any ordering-related bias and to promote uniform sample distribution across subsequent subsets. After shuffling, the dataset is divided into three subsets following an 80:10:10 split, corresponding to the training set (80%), validation set (10%), and test set (10%). The validation subset supports hyperparameter tuning and convergence monitoring during training, whereas the test subset is kept isolated and used only for final, unbiased evaluation on unseen data, thereby ensuring a fair assessment of generalization performance. All facial images are resized to a fixed spatial resolution of 224 × 224 pixels to match the input specifications of the ResNet-50 backbone employed for feature extraction within the landmark prediction pipeline.

4.3.1.4 DL based Feature Extraction and SVM Training

Facial landmark estimation in this study follows a two-stage hybrid strategy that combines deep learning with classical machine learning techniques. In the first stage, facial images undergo automatic feature extraction using a deep learning model designed for visual analysis. In the second stage, a support vector machine is trained on the extracted features to perform accurate regression of facial landmark coordinates. Within this framework, ResNet-50 is adopted as the feature extraction backbone due to its established effectiveness in deep residual learning. As illustrated in Figure 4.6, ResNet-50 does not operate as a classifier in this pipeline; instead, it functions as a high-level feature encoder, where activations from intermediate convolutional layers are obtained as discriminative facial representations for each dataset subset. These deep feature vectors encode complex facial structures and spatial relationships, and they are subsequently supplied to the SVM model to learn precise mappings between feature representations and landmark coordinate locations.

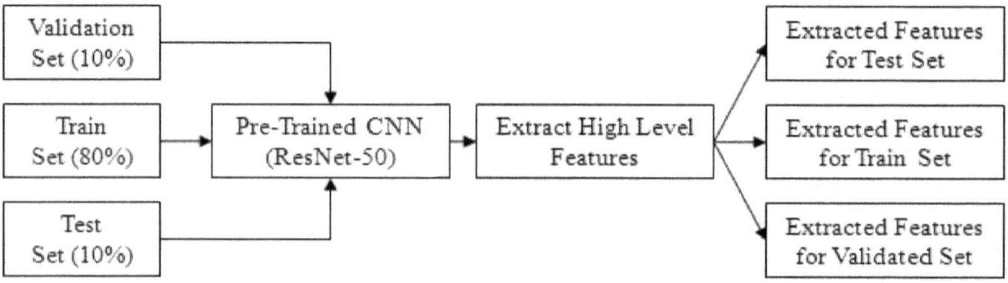

Figure 4.6. Illustration of high-level feature extraction operation using ResNet-50

Facial landmark detection in this work is modeled as a regression task, where the objective is to estimate the x and y coordinates of facial key points using extracted feature representations that encode detailed facial structure. For a given input image III, a feature vector $\text{F} \in \mathbb{R}^{\text{d}}$ is obtained from the ResNet-50 feature extractor and provided as input to the SVM model. The SVM learns a mapping function $f\colon \mathbb{R}^{d} \rightarrow \mathbb{R}^{2}$ that associates each feature vector with a corresponding landmark coordinate, which can be expressed as $\left(\hat{Y} = f(\text{F}) = WF + b\right)$ Here, $\hat{Y} = (\hat{x}, \hat{y})$ denotes the predicted facial landmark position, and WWW and bbb represent the learned weight matrix and bias term, respectively. The overall training workflow of the SVM-based regression process is illustrated in Figure 4.7.

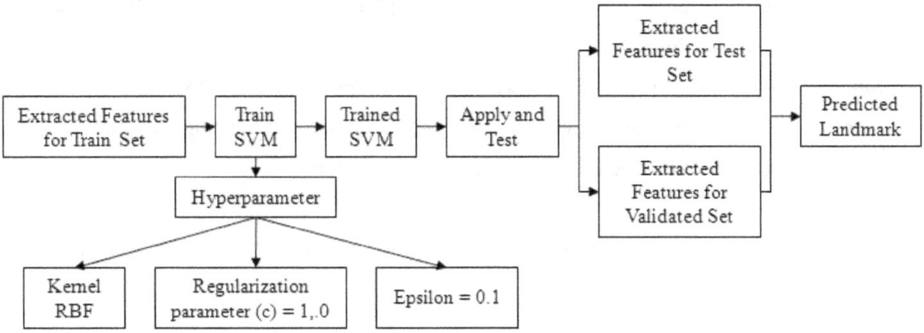

Figure 4.7. A schematic illustration of SVM training process

As illustrated in Figure 4.7, the deep feature vectors extracted from facial images are provided to the SVM model to learn reliable mappings between visual facial characteristics and their associated landmark coordinates. In this formulation, facial landmark detection is addressed as a supervised regression task, where the SVM establishes a relationship between high-dimensional deep feature representations and continuous coordinate values. In contrast to classification-oriented SVM formulations, the regression-based SVM focuses on estimating a function that minimizes prediction error within a predefined tolerance range, which supports stable learning behavior and produces accurate coordinate estimates for each facial landmark.

More specifically, the SVM estimates an optimal regression hyperplane within a transformed feature space by minimizing a regularized loss function that jointly controls prediction error and model complexity. This formulation allows the model to generalize to unseen facial variations rather than fitting only the training samples. However, learning this relationship directly in the original feature space remains inadequate because facial deformations introduced by pose variation, expression changes, and illumination differences exhibit strong non-linear behavior that cannot be effectively modeled using a simple linear mapping.

Since facial landmark estimation requires modeling non-linear relationships, SVM training is performed using a Radial Basis Function (RBF) kernel, also referred to as the Gaussian kernel (Liu et al., 2011). The kernel formulation enables the SVM to implicitly map deep feature vectors into a higher-dimensional space, where complex non-linear patterns become easier to approximate using linear regression boundaries, without explicitly computing the transformation. This implicit projection through the kernel trick reduces computational overhead when compared to explicit non-linear feature expansion, which supports efficient execution under real-time landmark prediction constraints. The mathematical expression of the RBF kernel is given as follows:

$$K(F_i, F_j) = \exp\left(-\gamma\, ||F_i - F_j||^2\right) \tag{4.7}$$

From Equation 4.7, $K(F_i, F_j)$ denotes the similarity measure computed between two feature vectors, where γ\gammaγ is a tunable hyperparameter that regulates the width of the Gaussian RBF kernel, and $||F_i - F_j||^2$ represents the squared Euclidean distance between the corresponding feature vectors. The value of γ directly controls the locality of influence of individual training samples, where smaller values allow broader generalization and larger values emphasize local feature interactions. Through appropriate adjustment of this parameter, the model achieves precise landmark regression while preventing unnecessary increase in model complexity.

Another important hyperparameter in the SVM formulation is the regularization parameter C, which governs the balance between minimizing training error and controlling model complexity in order to reduce overfitting. In addition, a tolerance parameter ε\varepsilonε is introduced to define an acceptable margin of error for regression-based prediction of facial landmark coordinates. This tolerance allows small deviations between predicted and true landmark positions without imposing excessive penalty, which supports stable learning behavior. Accordingly, the objective function for the SVM-based facial landmark prediction model, as described by Ye et al. (2020), is formulated as follows:

$$[\min_{W,b} \frac{1}{2} ||W||^2 + C \sum_{i=1}^{N} \max(0, |Y_i - \widehat{Y}_i| - \varepsilon)] \tag{4.8}$$

From Equation 4.8, Y_i and $\widehat{Y}_i$ denote the ground-truth and predicted landmark coordinates, respectively, and NNN represents the total number of training samples. The term $\max(0, |Y_i - \widehat{Y}_i| - \varepsilon)$ enforces the ε-insensitive tolerance margin, which ensures that prediction errors falling within the specified margin are not penalized during training.

After training, the SVM model is evaluated on both the validation and test datasets using Mean Squared Error as the primary performance measure. The use of MSE is appropriate in this context because facial landmark detection is formulated as a regression task, where the objective is to minimize the deviation between predicted and actual coordinate values. Mean Squared Error is widely applied for assessing regression model performance, as it quantifies the average squared difference between estimated and true outputs and provides a clear numerical indication of prediction accuracy (Chakraborty and Kumar, 2022). The mathematical formulation of MSE is presented in Equation 4.9 below.

$$MSE = \frac{1}{n} \sum_{i=1}^{n} (y_i - \widehat{y}_i)^2 \tag{4.9}$$

From Equ 4.9, Where, n is the number of samples (i.e., number of landmark coordinates, which is 136 for 68 landmarks), y_i denotes the ground truth, and $\widehat{y}_i$ indicates the predicted value (predicted landmark coordinate)

4.3.2 Behavioral Cues detection

After the SVM model is trained, it is applied for facial landmark detection, and the predicted landmarks are then used to extract behavioral cues by measuring eye openness through the Eye Aspect Ratio and detecting yawning events through the Mouth Aspect Ratio, both of which represent important indicators of driver drowsiness and fatigue (Sri Mounika et al., 2022). The computation of EAR is performed to determine whether the eyes are in an open or closed state, which serves as a direct visual cue of reduced alertness. The mathematical formulation of EAR is given in Equation 4.10 below.

$$EAR = \frac{||P_2 - P_6|| + ||P_3 - P_5||}{2 \times ||P_1 - P_4||} \tag{4.10}$$

Here, P_1 and P_4 correspond to the horizontal eye landmark points, whereas P_2 and P_6 alog with P_3 and P_5, represent the vertical eye landmark pairs. The term , || P_a - P_b|| denotes the Euclidean distance measured between landmark points P_a and P_b. The Eye Aspect Ratio remains relatively stable when the eyes are open and exhibits a sharp decrease during blinking or prolonged eye closure, which makes it a reliable measure for detecting eye closure events associated with drowsiness. In a similar manner, the Mouth Aspect Ratio is used to identify yawning behavior, which represents another important visual cue of driver fatigue. The mathematical expression for MAR is provided in Equation 4.11 below.

$$\text{MAR} = \frac{||P_2 - P_8|| + ||P_3 - P_7|| + ||P_4 - P_6||}{2 \times ||P_1 - P_5||} \quad (4.11)$$

In this formulation, , P1 and P5 denote the horizontal corner points of the mouth, whereas P2 and P8 represent the outer vertical landmarks corresponding to the upper and lower lips. Similarly, P3 and P7 indicate the middle vertical lip landmarks, and P4 and P6 correspond to the inner vertical lip points. The term || P_a - P_b|| refers to the Euclidean distance computed between any two landmark points P_a and P_b, which quantifies the degree of mouth opening required for accurate yawning detection.

Apart from these geometric cues (EAR and MAR), the proposed framework incorporates a DL-based behavioral cue that further enhances detection reliability. Specifically, a CNN model developed in the previous chapter is employed to analyze eye-region images and predict the driver's eye status (open or closed) directly from visual features. The model was trained on a large-scale dataset containing more than 10,000 facial images, manually annotated into alert and drowsy eye states based on visible eye closure characteristics, ensuring reliable supervision for binary classification. During real-time execution, the eye region is extracted from each video frame and passed through the trained CNN model, which outputs a drowsiness probability score. This score is treated as an additional behavioral indicator and evaluated against a predefined threshold to support the final drowsiness decision. By integrating geometric features (EAR, MAR) with DL-based eye state classification, the proposed system jointly exploits localized spatial cues and learned global visual representations, resulting in a more robust and comprehensive driver monitoring solution under real-world driving conditions.

4.3.3 Multi-Stage Decision Logic

To improve the accuracy and dependability of drowsiness detection, the proposed system applies a multi-stage decision fusion mechanism that integrates deep learning predictions with geometric feature thresholds, specifically Eye Aspect Ratio and Mouth Aspect Ratio. This fusion approach combines CNN-derived probability scores with handcrafted geometric indicators, which helps limit both false-positive and false-negative detections. The system performs continuous monitoring of EAR, MAR, and the CNN confidence output, and an alert is triggered only when one or more of these indicators consistently exceed predefined threshold values across a fixed number of successive frames. This temporal validation ensures stable and reliable detection behavior under real driving conditions. The exact threshold settings and fusion rules used in this framework are summarized in Table 4.1.

Table 4.1. Multi-stage decision fusion thresholds

Metric	Purpose	Threshold	Consecutive Frames	Evaluation Criteria
EAR	Detects prolonged eye closure	0.26	15	Trigger alert if EAR < 0.26 for 15 consecutive frames
MAR	Identifies yawning frequency	0.05	20	Record yawn if MAR > 0.05 for 20 consecutive frames
CNN Probability	Measures overall likelihood of drowsiness	0.35	15	Trigger alert if CNN probability < 0.30 for 15 consecutive frames

In this framework, Eye Aspect Ratio (EAR) is applied to monitor prolonged eye closure, Mouth Aspect Ratio (MAR) is used to detect yawning activity, and the CNN probability score directly estimates the overall likelihood of driver drowsiness based on learned facial representations. The combined use of these indicators ensures that short-duration events, such as natural blinking or brief facial movements occurring within a single frame, do not lead to false alerts, thereby improving overall system robustness. To further strengthen reliability, a rolling counter mechanism is introduced to record consecutive frames in which EAR, MAR, or the CNN probability surpass their respective threshold values. Each counter is updated at every frame, so that only sustained drowsiness-related patterns contribute to the final decision. This approach suppresses false alarms caused by temporary changes in facial expression, lighting conditions, or head motion. When any counter exceeds its predefined limit, the system activates an alert and records the event for further analysis. The configured threshold values and counter parameters are summarized in Table 4.2, and the operational workflow of the counter-based decision logic is illustrated in Figure 4.8.

Table 4.2. Summary of Counter Mechanism

Counter	Purpose	Threshold	Consecutive Frames	Evaluation Criteria
EAR Counter	Tracks frames with EAR below the threshold	0.26	15	Increment if EAR < 0.26, reset if EAR >= 0.26. Trigger alert if counter exceeds 15.
MAR Counter	Tracks frames with MAR above the threshold	0.05	20	Increment if MAR > 0.05, reset if MAR <= 0.05. Record yawn if counter exceeds 20.
CNN Counter	Tracks frames with CNN probability below threshold	0.3	15	Increment if CNN probability < 0.3, reset if probability >= 0.3. Trigger alert if counter exceeds 15.

The threshold values and consecutive-frame limits reported in Table 4.2 were not arbitrarily chosen but were determined through empirical analysis and iterative experimentation during system development. Initial threshold ranges for EAR, MAR, and CNN probability were selected based on commonly reported values in the literature for eye closure and yawning detection and were subsequently refined using validation experiments on real-time video sequences. The selected EAR threshold (0.26) corresponds to a clear separation between open and closed eye states observed across multiple subjects, while the MAR threshold (0.05) reliably captures sustained mouth opening associated with yawning rather than normal speech or facial motion. The consecutive-frame limits were introduced to incorporate temporal persistence, ensuring that only sustained behavioral patterns trigger alerts. These values were tuned to balance detection responsiveness and false-alarm suppression, particularly under transient events such as normal blinking, brief head movements, or illumination changes. The CNN probability threshold was calibrated using validation data to reflect low-confidence predictions consistently associated with drowsy eye states. Overall, this empirically guided thresholding and counter-based design provides a practical engineering trade-off between sensitivity and robustness for real-time driver monitoring.

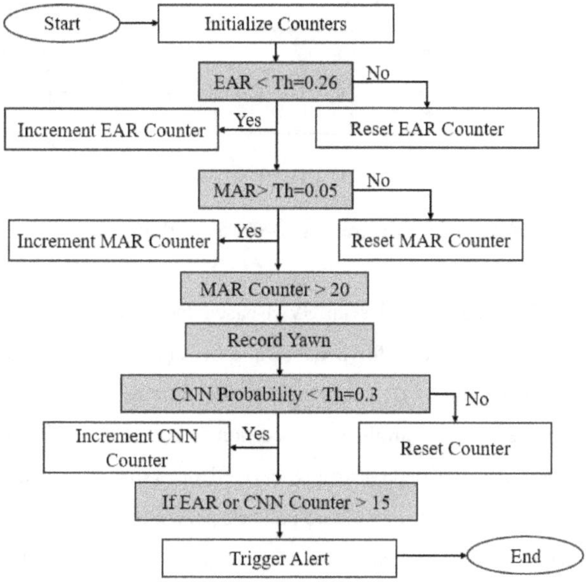

Figure 4.8. Illustrates workflow of proposed counter mechanism

4.4 REAL-WORLD WORKING SCENARIO OF THE PROPOSED METHODOLOGY

The complete operational flow of the proposed integrated framework is shown in Figure 4.9. The system receives real-time video input from a camera placed to continuously capture the driver's facial region during driving. To maintain a balance between computational efficiency and real-time performance, the system processes only every third frame from the video stream, which reduces processing load without adversely affecting detection reliability. Each selected frame is then resized to match the input specifications required by the deep learning components of the framework.

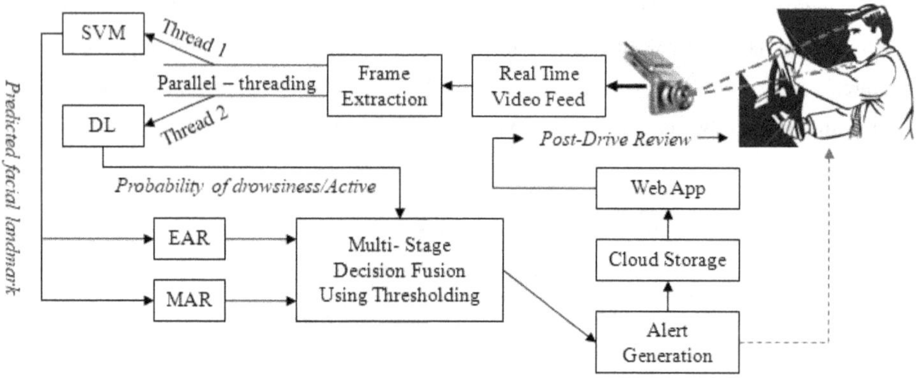

Figure 4.9. Illustrates real-world working scenario

In parallel, the system applies an SVM-based facial landmark detection module to identify key facial points required for behavioral assessment. The estimated landmarks are used to calculate EAR and MAR measures, which represent eye closure behavior and yawning activity, respectively. A multi-level decision fusion mechanism then combines these geometric indicators with the deep learning–derived drowsiness probability score, and an alert is issued only when drowsiness-related patterns persist over several consecutive frames. This temporal verification limits false alerts caused by brief facial movements or short-term behavioral changes. All detected drowsiness events are recorded and transmitted to a cloud-based platform, which allows post-drive analysis through a web-based interface. The complete framework emphasizes efficient execution, reduced computational demand, and scalability, thereby supporting practical real-world deployment with a low false-alarm rate.

4.5 RESULT AND DISCUSSION

The design and implementation of the proposed system were performed using the Python programming language, with model execution carried out through the Anaconda distribution on a Windows 10 platform. This section presents a detailed performance analysis of the developed driver drowsiness detection framework, focusing on its effectiveness and reliability under the defined experimental setup.

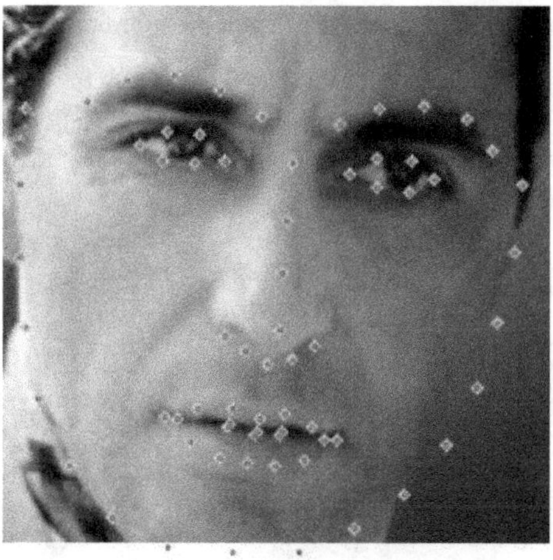

Figure 4.10. Visual analysis of the predicted (green) and actual (red) landmark from test set

Figure 4.10 presents the performance evaluation of the proposed SVM-based facial landmark detection system. The analysis is carried on the test sample image and it can be seen that predicted landmark coordinates in green color closly matches to the ground truth (red) that demonstrates model's capability in accurately identifying key facial features.

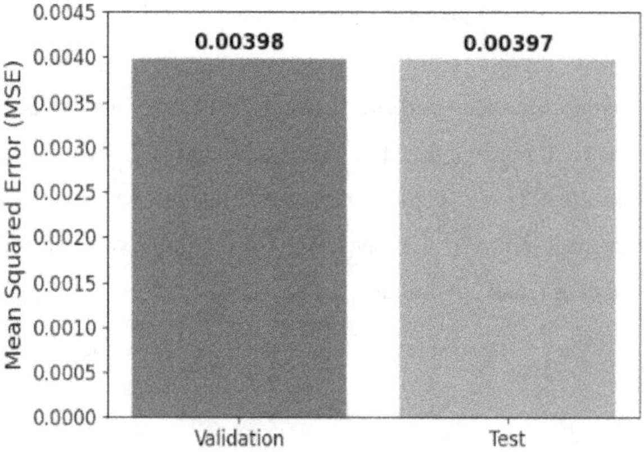

Figure 4.11. MSE analysis

The MSE analysis, shown in Figure 4.11, indicates minimal error rates on both validation and test datasets, with values of 0.00398 and 0.00397, respectively. These low values reflect the model's high accuracy in landmark coordinate prediction, with negligible variance between validation and test performance. Such consistency affirms the generalizability of the model and supports its robustness in real-time facial landmark estimation tasks.

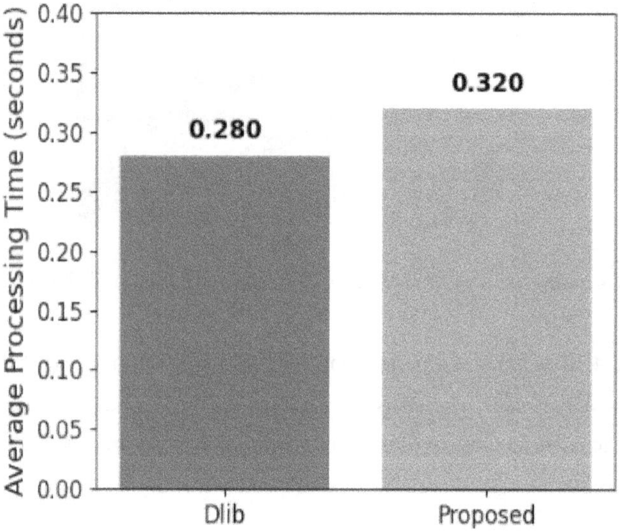

Figure 4.12. Process time analysis

The processing time comparison between Dlib and the proposed SVM model, depicted in Figure 4.12 reveals that the proposed approach incurs a slight increase in computational time (0.320s vs. 0.280s) due to the additional feature extraction phase. However, this marginal delay is compensated for by improved robustness in landmark prediction under varying facial conditions.

Figure 4.13. Output Frame 1

The above Figure 4.13 displays an example output frame from the proposed hybrid drowsiness detection system. The output shown in Figure 4.13 simultaneously visualizes the predictions made from multiple behavioral cues through CNN-based classification, the EAR, and MAR outputs along with superimposed visual facial landmarks. First, since this is a learning model, the probability refers to the current confidence score predicted by the CNN model (1.00). This indicates that the deep learning model does not detect any indication of drowsiness in the current frame that is defined as not drowsy class by the trained model. Secondly, the annotation "EAR (0.19)" indicates the case of 0.19 for the EAR which is below the previously defined EAR threshold of 0.26 for the study as defined in Chapter 3. Therefore, when the EAR is above 0.26 it typically indicates that the eyes is partially closed. Again, the framework's design indicates that it will not register an alert until the EAR has dropped below the threshold for 15 consecutive frames, so brief blinks (typically < 1 second) or temporary occlusions can be eliminated. The MAR is measured at 0.02, which is below the yawning threshold of 0.05, therefore there is no yawning behavior detected in the current frame.

Figure 4.14. Output frame 2

The frame shown in **Figure 4.14** illustrates a scenario in which the CNN model outputs a drowsiness probability of **1.00**, indicating an alert state. The EAR value is **0.25**, which is marginally below the predefined threshold of **0.26**, suggesting partially open eyes but not sustained eye closure. The MAR value is **0.06**, which exceeds the yawning threshold of **0.05**, and therefore indicates a yawning event. The annotation *"Yawns recorded: 1"* reflects the persistence of mouth opening across consecutive frames, rather than a single-frame mouth movement. It is important to note that a yawn is not identified from a single frame alone, as brief or partial mouth openings may occur during normal speech or facial movement. Instead, yawning is detected only when the MAR value consistently exceeds the threshold over a predefined number of consecutive frames, as defined by the counter mechanism. In this frame, the yawn count corresponds to a yawning event that began in previous frames and persisted into the current frame. No alert is generated because the CNN model indicates an alert state and the yawning event has not yet reached the alert-triggering condition.

Figure 4.15. Output frame 3

In Figure 4.15, the presented frame reflects strong evidence to support detection of drowsiness. The CNN model reports a probability of 0.00. This confirms the drowsy state. The EAR value is 0.14, which is well below the threshold of 0.26, suggesting closed eyes; the MAR value is 0.07, which suggests a yawning behavior is active, and one yawn has been recorded. There is a "Wake Up!" alert with sound. The figure depicts the drowsy state being recordable for alert in multiple states and supports a high-risk drowsy condition by both the CNN reporting drowsiness and the behavioral metrics for drowsiness.

The analysis of Figure 4.16 reflects another frame that the CNN model identifies a drowsy state with a probability of 0.00. The EAR value is extremely low at 0.08, suggesting the eyes are fully closed. The MAR value is 0.03 which did not exhibit yawning for this frame. Despite the absence of a new yawn, the previously recorded count remains one. A **"Wake Up!"** alert is displayed due to persistent eye closure and low CNN confidence, highlighting continued drowsiness.

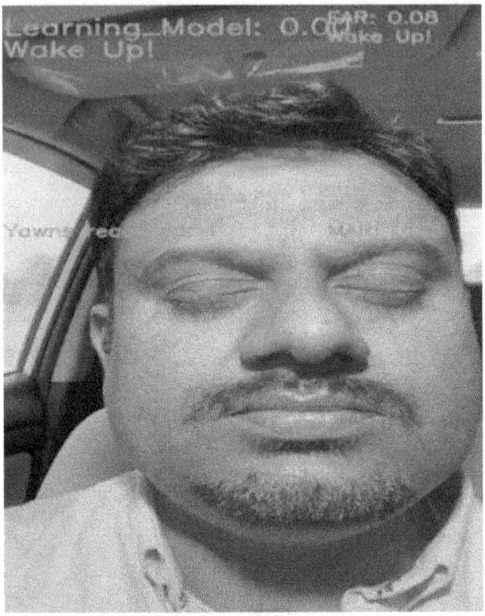

Figure 4.16. Output frame 4

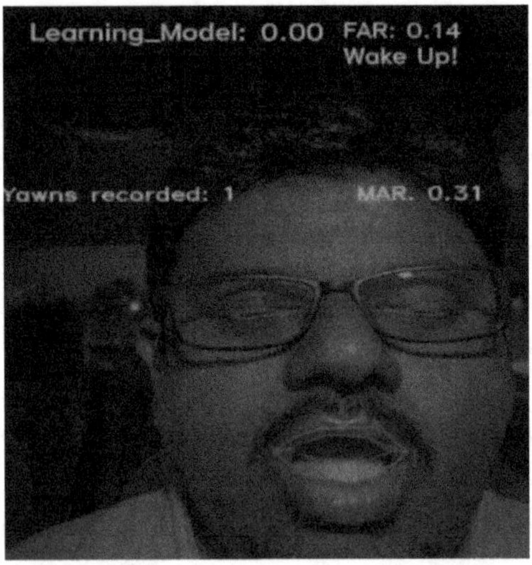

Figure 4.17. Output frame 5 in night scene

The results shown in Figure 4.17 show a severe drowsy state where the CNN model predicts drowsy with a probability of 0.00 in the night scene. The EAR is 0.14 indicating eye closure, and the MAR is extremely elevated at 0.31 indicating a highly probable Yawn event. The one yawn that is captured will cause the system to process a "Wake Up!" sound alert. This frame captures several key high-risk behavioral signals that confirm the driver's drowsiness state. Table 4.3 provides a concise summary of results and findings with respect to the outcomes discussed.

Table 4.3. Summary of the outcomes

Frame	Learning Model Probability	EAR	MAR	Yawns Recorded	Alert Status	Outcome Findings
Frame 1	1.00	0.19	0.02	0	No Alerts	EAR below threshold but not for 15 consecutive frames.
Frame 2	1.00	0.25	0.06	1	No Alerts	MAR above threshold one yawn recorded.
Frame 3	0.00	0.14	0.07	1	Wake Up Alert	EAR well below threshold, CNN probability detects drowsiness.
Frame 4	0.00	0.08	0.03	1	Wake Up Alert	EAR well below thresholds, no yawing but CNN probability confirms drowsiness
Frame 5	0.00	0.14	0.31	1	Wake Up Alert	EAR below threshold, high MAR indicating yawing, CNN probability detects drowsiness.

It should be noted that direct benchmarking of the proposed framework against existing studies is not feasible because of the distinctive nature of the adopted hybrid design, which integrates an SVM-based facial landmark detection model with deep learning–driven behavioral analysis using EAR, MAR, and threshold-based decision logic for real-time driver state monitoring. Most existing driver drowsiness detection approaches relied either on standalone deep learning models or on traditional feature-based methods, without jointly combining multiple behavioral cues within a unified hybrid framework, and they were not evaluated on a comparable custom real-time dataset with synchronized multi-metric thresholding. In addition, differences in dataset composition, experimental configurations, and evaluation metrics further limit the validity of direct comparisons. Therefore, the performance analysis presented in this section is conducted relative to internal baseline configurations and system-specific threshold settings, with emphasis on real-time execution behavior, robustness of facial landmark localization, effectiveness of behavioral cue fusion, and responsiveness of alert generation under live operating conditions. This evaluation strategy provides a practical assessment of the proposed system's real-world effectiveness and establishes a foundation for future work involving standardized datasets and benchmarking protocols.

4.6 SUMMARY

This study presented the design, implementation, and evaluation of an advanced driver drowsiness detection framework that combines machine learning–based facial landmark estimation with deep learning–based eye-state classification, together with behavioral indicators derived from Eye Aspect Ratio and Mouth Aspect Ratio. The main aim of the proposed approach was to integrate machine learning and deep learning models within an adaptive multi-level decision mechanism that continuously assesses driver alertness and generates timely warnings under drowsy conditions. Experimental validation using real-time video streams showed that the developed framework detects drowsiness effectively by analyzing eye and mouth behavior, while substantially reducing false-positive alerts through temporal thresholding and decision-level fusion. The evaluation was performed under varied real-world driving conditions, including changes in illumination, head orientation, and facial appearance, where the deep learning component supported stable performance in scenarios that typically degrade purely geometric approaches. Although the proposed system demonstrated strong reliability, the framework in this chapter primarily emphasizes eye and mouth cues and does not explicitly model broader inter-subject variability or microsleep-related temporal patterns. These limitations are addressed in the following chapter by extending the system with multi-feature integration and a fuzzy logic–based decision framework to improve adaptability under dynamic driving environments.

CHAPTER-5

FUZZY-BASED ADAPTIVE DECISION FRAMEWORK FOR REAL-TIME DROWSINESS DETECTION

5.1 INTRODUCTION

Driver sleepiness is a major cause of road accidents and creates a strong need for reliable early detection systems. Many existing drowsiness detections approaches primarily rely on eye closure analysis using the Eye Aspect Ratio (EAR); however, such methods often suffer from considerable false positives and false negatives due to underlying inter-individual anatomical variations. In particular, differences related to race, eye shape, blinking mechanisms, and facial structure are not adequately accounted for, which can lead to incorrect classification of a driver's alertness state. In addition, certain conditions such as microsleep episodes or forced eye-opening behavior may not be easily observable through simple eye-closure metrics alone. As a result, there exists a need for a more flexible detection mechanism that can incorporate multiple indicators and support adaptive real-time drowsiness assessment. One of the key challenges in driver monitoring is to accurately distinguish fatigue, pre-drowsy, and fully drowsy states without generating alerts either too late or unnecessarily early.

Based on the analysis of existing studies, the following limitations are evident in current systems: (i) EAR alone is insufficient to capture early and transitional pre-drowsiness stages; (ii) yawning information derived from MAR introduces additional behavioral context but does not independently provide reliable confidence; (iii) indicators related to microsleep events are largely ignored; and (iv) blink duration, which can reflect forced eye-opening behavior, has received limited attention alongside conventional EAR- and MAR-based approaches. To address these limitations, this chapter introduces a multi-feature fuzzy logic–based drowsiness detection framework. Fuzzy logic refers to a rule-based reasoning approach that enables decision-making under uncertainty by allowing partial membership between states, rather than enforcing rigid binary classifications. Using this paradigm, multiple physiological and behavioral indicators, including EAR, MAR, head position, eyeball movement, and blink duration all are jointly evaluated to support adaptive and context-aware inference. Such a fuzzy-based multi-feature integration enables gradual modeling of driver alertness transitions and facilitates the early detection of pre-drowsiness, thereby allowing timely and proportionate alert generation ahead of critical drowsy states.

5.2 RESEARCH PROBLEM

Most current drowsiness detection systems are built using a fixed threshold system based on EAR. This is a limitation, as fixed values do not consider the natural variation in shape and size of eyes among different drivers. A naturally smaller eyed driver, when compared to a larger-eyed driver, may never be given a drowsy indicator and risk an accident whereas the larger eyed driver may receive drowsy indicators prematurely. This inherent variability makes technology less reliable for the average user. A much more accurate system should be able to change according to the user's personal variability and real-time driving condition factors.

Another major limitation of most existing drowsiness detection systems is their inability to detect microsleep events. Microsleeps are brief, involuntary episodes of reduced awareness during which a driver may appear to be awake despite experiencing momentary lapses in attention. Such events are often characterized by rapid downward eye movements, short head nodding motions, or a temporary loss of gaze fixation. Systems that rely solely on EAR-based eye closure detection may fail to capture these events, particularly in cases where the driver's eyes remain partially open but cognitive engagement is lost. Without monitoring eyeball movement and head position, short-duration lapses in attention can remain undetected.

In addition, some drivers consciously attempt to counteract drowsiness by forcing their eyelids open despite significant fatigue. This behavior can lead to false negative detections, where the system incorrectly classifies the driver as alert based on eye openness alone, even though other physiological and behavioral cues indicate drowsiness. As a result, reliance on EAR alone is insufficient for robust driver state estimation. A reliable detection system must therefore extend beyond simple eye closure metrics and incorporate complementary indicators such as blink duration, eye movement dynamics, and head tilt in order to accurately characterize the driver's alertness state.

Another significant challenge concerns real-time processing limitations, particularly when deployment targets embedded automotive platforms. Many existing deep learning–based drowsiness detection methods require high computational resources, which restricts their practical use on low-power hardware such as Raspberry Pi or Jetson Nano devices. Therefore, a lightweight yet dependable alternative is necessary to maintain an effective balance between computational efficiency and detection accuracy. Fuzzy logic provides such an alternative by supporting decision-making under uncertainty through rule-based reasoning rather than computationally expensive numerical optimization. Instead of applying rigid thresholds or binary outputs, fuzzy logic models gradual transitions between alertness states and allows partial membership across multiple fatigue levels at the same time. This characteristic aligns well with real-world drowsiness behavior, where fatigue develops progressively and sensor observations remain inherently imprecise. As a result, fuzzy logic enables adaptive and context-aware reasoning with minimal computational overhead, which makes it suitable for embedded real-time driver monitoring applications. Based on these considerations, the primary challenges addressed in this chapter are summarized in Table 5.1.

Table 5.1. Highlights for the critical issues in existing drowsiness detection systems

References	Problem	Description
Sahayadhas et al. (2012); Dziuda et al. (2021); Murata et al. (2022)	Fixed EAR-based detection is insufficient	Eye Aspect Ratio–based methods are sensitive to inter-individual anatomical variations in eye shape and size, which can lead to false positives for drivers with naturally small eyes and false negatives for drivers with larger eyes.
Altameem et al. (2021); Kassem et al. (2021); Sri Mounika et al. (2022)	Lack of early warning mechanism	Many systems detect drowsiness only after sustained eye closure, failing to capture early fatigue indicators such as yawning frequency, gradual head tilting, and prolonged blinking.
Doudou et al. (2023); Nojiri et al. (2019); Murugan et al. (2023)	Microsleep detection is missing	Brief involuntary sleep episodes (microsleeps), characterized by rapid downward eye movement and short head nodding, are often not detected by systems relying solely on eye closure metrics.
Ngxande et al. (2020); Kassem et al.	False negatives due to forced	Drivers may consciously force their eyes open despite being drowsy, resulting in misclassification

(2021); Ye et al. (2021)	eye opening	of alertness when detection relies only on eye openness measurements.
Abulkhair et al. (2015); Ramzan et al. (2019); Lamaazi et al. (2023)	Need for real-time, lightweight processing	Many deep learning-based approaches demand high computational resources, limiting their applicability for real-time deployment on embedded automotive platforms such as Raspberry Pi or Jetson Nano.

To address the aforementioned research challenges, the proposed fuzzy logic-based approach offers a context-aware decision-making framework that significantly reduces false alarms by integrating multiple behavioral and physiological features for the analysis of pre-drowsiness states. Unlike traditional fixed threshold-based models, the proposed system employs an adaptive rule base and a customized alert mechanism, thereby facilitating more reliable detection and enhancing driver engagement.

5.3 PROPOSED FRAMEWOKR DESIGN

The proposed research introduces a multi-feature computational framework based on fuzzy logic for real-time driver drowsiness detection. The main objective of the system is to support robust, adaptive, and early identification of drowsiness conditions so that timely warnings can be issued before the driver reaches a critical fatigue state. The framework is designed to operate directly on live video streams, which allows continuous observation of the driver and prompt alert generation based on the estimated alertness level. The overall system structure is carefully organized to maintain a balance between detection accuracy and computational efficiency, which ensures feasibility for deployment on low-cost embedded automotive platforms. To achieve this balance, the framework is divided into clearly defined computational modules, where each module is responsible for extracting or processing a specific behavioral or physiological cue related to driver alertness. In particular, the framework includes: (i) a facial landmark detection module that extracts stable geometric key points from the driver's face; (ii) a feature computation module that derives quantitative indicators such as eye closure status using EAR, mouth opening using MAR, blink duration, head position, eyeball movement, and abrupt EAR variations associated with forced wakefulness; and (iii) a fuzzy inference and decision module that integrates all extracted features through an adaptive rule base to estimate the driver's drowsiness level under uncertainty. Each module is explained in detail in the following subsections, where the mathematical formulation, implementation approach, and behavioral significance of the extracted features are systematically discussed. By integrating these components within a fuzzy logic–based decision framework, the proposed system supports context-aware and adaptive reasoning, reduces unnecessary alerts, and improves reliability under ambiguous real-world driving conditions. The overall schematic representation of the proposed framework is shown in Figure 5.1.

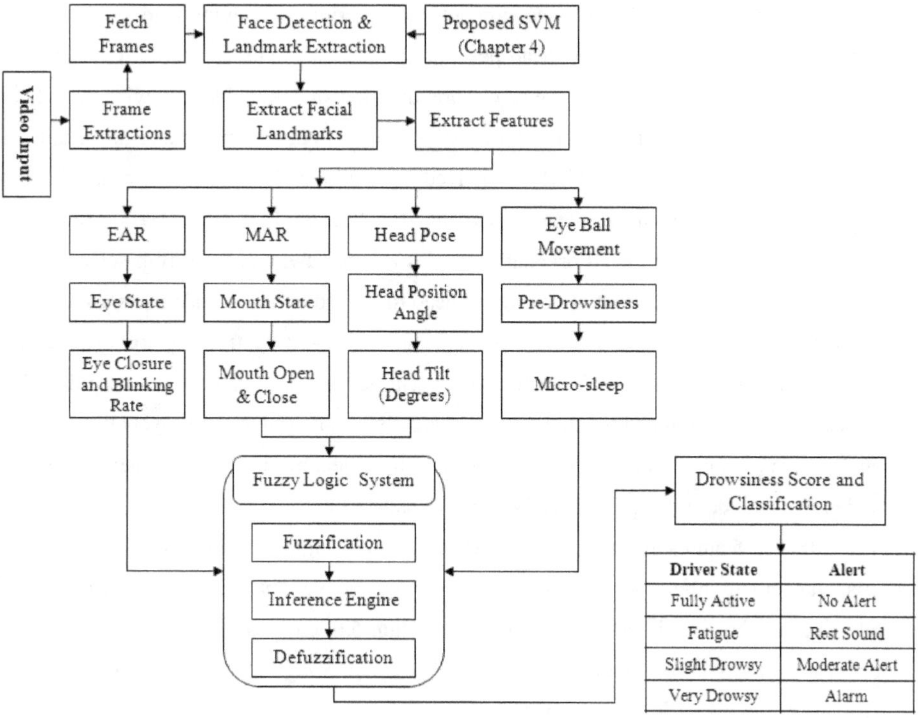

Figure 5.1. Schematic illustration of the proposed fuzzy logic system

As illustrated in Figure 5.1, the proposed computational framework is composed of well-defined and functionally independent modules, each designed to perform a specific task in the overall driver drowsiness detection process. The framework follows a real-time facial analysis process, where all modules operate synchronously and exchange information in a tightly integrated manner to ensure low-latency decision making. The system takes a live video stream as input and extracts frames sequentially. Each frame undergoes preprocessing that includes resizing to 224 × 224 pixels and conversion to a single-channel intensity image, ensuring consistency with subsequent feature extraction stages. The preprocessed frame is then passed to the facial landmark prediction module, where an SVM-based landmark detector, introduced and validated in Chapter 4, is employed to extract precise facial key points. These landmarks serve as the geometric foundation for all subsequent behavioral feature computations.

The feature extraction stage computes four critical behavioral and physiological parameters, namely EAR, MAR, head pose, and eyeball movement. The EAR is computed from eye landmarks to quantify eye closure duration and blinking behavior, which are directly associated with fatigue; the formulation and computation procedure are detailed in Section 5.5.1. Similarly, the MAR is derived from mouth landmarks to measure mouth opening and detect yawning events, as explained in Section 5.5.2. Head pose estimation is performed by computing head orientation angles (pitch, yaw, and roll) from selected facial landmarks, enabling detection of downward head tilt linked to reduced alertness, as described in Section 5.5.4. In addition, eyeball movement is analyzed by tracking iris displacement across consecutive frames to capture gaze shifts, nodding behavior, and microsleep indicators. The computation strategy and underlying algorithms for eyeball movement analysis are presented in Section 5.5.5. Together, these features provide complementary local and global cues describing the driver's vigilance state.

The extracted features are subsequently fed into a fuzzy logic–based decision system, where crisp numerical inputs are transformed into linguistic variables and evaluated using an adaptive rule base. This process, detailed in Section 5.6, enables the system to classify the driver's alertness into four distinct states: *Fully Active*, *Fatigue*, *Slightly Drowsy*, and *Very Drowsy*.

Based on the inferred state, a corresponding alert mechanism is activated. No alert is issued in the fully active state, a mild rest alert is triggered during fatigue, a moderate warning is issued for slight drowsiness, and an emergency alarm is activated in severe drowsiness conditions to prompt immediate corrective action. By integrating multi-feature behavioral analysis with fuzzy logic–based inference, the proposed system achieves adaptive, context-aware drowsiness detection, significantly reducing false alarms and improving reliability under real-world driving conditions. The next subsection discusses the modeling assumptions that underpin the proposed framework.

5.4 MODELING ASSUMPTIONS AND INITIAL HYPOTHESES

In order to design a reliable and adaptive drowsiness detection system, the proposed research work establishes several modeling assumptions based on both physiological and behavioral evidence. These initial hypotheses support the architecture of the proposed fuzzy logic framework and ensure that the system effectively captures pre-drowsiness states, microsleeps, and forced alertness, leading to accurate and timely warnings.

5.4.1 EAR is necessary but alone is not sufficient

The Eye Aspect Ratio (EAR) is a widely used geometric indicator for estimating eye openness and blink behavior in vision-based drowsiness detection systems. However, the reliability of EAR as a sole indicator is limited due to inter-individual anatomical variability, which can lead to inconsistent thresholding across drivers. Although EAR captures eyelid dynamics effectively, its absolute value is influenced by facial anatomy rather than fatigue alone, making it insufficient as a standalone measure for robust drowsiness detection.

1) Anatomical source of EAR variability: The observed inter-individual variation in EAR does not arise from differences in eyeball size, as the adult human eyeball diameter remains relatively constant (approximately 23–24 mm). Instead, variability originates primarily from differences in the palpebral fissure, defined as the visible opening between the upper and lower eyelids. Ophthalmological studies report that palpebral fissure height and width vary significantly among individuals due to eyelid morphology, age, ethnicity, and facial structure. Reported vertical palpebral fissure heights range approximately from 8.5 mm to 11.5 mm in healthy adults, despite similar eyeball dimensions (Srinivasan et al., 2015). As a result, a driver with a naturally smaller palpebral fissure may exhibit consistently lower EAR values even in an alert state.

2) Implications for drowsiness detection systems: Due to this anatomical variability, fixed EAR thresholds cannot generalize reliably across drivers. A driver with a larger palpebral fissure may retain relatively high EAR values even under fatigue, whereas another driver may cross drowsiness thresholds prematurely despite being alert. This limitation increases the likelihood of false positives and false negatives when EAR is used in isolation. Therefore, EAR should be treated as a necessary but insufficient indicator and must be integrated with complementary behavioral features, such as blink duration, yawning, head pose, and eyeball movement, to achieve reliable and adaptive drowsiness detection.

5.4.2 Multi-feature integration enhances detection robustness

Reliable drowsiness assessment depends on the integration of multiple behavioral features, including Mouth Aspect Ratio, head position, eyeball movement, blink duration, and variations in Eye Aspect Ratio. The combined use of these indicators improves detection reliability by limiting false-positive decisions and allows the system to differentiate between fatigue-related conditions such as early fatigue, pre-drowsiness, and deep drowsiness states.

5.4.3 Feature combinations enable early and reliable detection

The combination of moderate reductions in EAR, increased MAR, slightly prolonged blinks, and mild downward head tilt typically signifies the onset of fatigue before critical drowsiness occurs. On the other hand, significant reductions in EAR, frequent yawning (high MAR), and strong downward head tilt indicate a high likelihood of microsleeps or imminent loss of awareness.

5.4.4 Head position is a sensitive indicator of drowsiness progression

An upright head position generally indicates alertness. The transition from a slight to a strong downward head tilt is a reliable marker for escalating fatigue and the onset of deep drowsiness or microsleeps.

- Upright head position → Driver is fully active.
- Slight downward tilt → Indicates early fatigue.
- Strong downward tilt → Suggests the driver is entering deep drowsiness or microsleep.

5.4.5 Eyeball movement patterns reflect microsleep episodes

In alert states, eye movements are primarily horizontal as drivers scan their environment. During pre-drowsiness, movements slow and may shift vertically. Similarly, sudden downward shifts in eyeball movement, even in the absence of low EAR, suggest the onset of microsleep episodes.

- In normal conditions, eyeball movement is mostly horizontal (left-right shifts to check mirrors, surroundings).
- In pre-drowsiness states, eyeball movement slows down and becomes more vertical (nodding off motion).
- A sudden downward shift in eye movement, even when EAR is medium or high, suggests a driver is struggling to stay awake.

5.4.6 Blink duration reveals drowsiness severity

The study considers that the sustained blinks lasting 1–2 seconds are indicative of mild drowsiness, while blinks exceeding 2 seconds reflect severe drowsiness. Additionally, frequent and abrupt transitions between low and high EAR may signal forced eye opening, an attempt to mask drowsiness.

- If blinks last between 1–2 seconds, the driver is considered slightly drowsy, as such durations exceed normal reflexive blinking and indicate early fatigue.
- If blinks last more than 2 seconds, the driver is considered very drowsy, as prolonged eyelid closure strongly correlates with microsleep onset and loss of situational awareness.
- If frequent transitions between low and high EAR values occur, the driver is considered to be forcing eye opening, thereby reflecting a compensatory effort to remain awake despite underlying drowsiness.

5.4.7 Sudden increases in ear signal forced alertness

A rapid rise in EAR following a period of low EAR suggests the driver is consciously forcing their eyes open to counteract fatigue. If this is accompanied by yawning, head tilting, or prolonged blinks, the underlying drowsy state persists despite apparent alertness. These modeling assumptions constitute the foundation of our fuzzy logic-based approach, enabling context-aware, real-time drowsiness detection that adapts to variable driver behaviors and environmental conditions.

- A sudden EAR increase after a low EAR period suggests the driver is forcing their eyes open.

- If this is combined with yawning, head tilting, or prolonged blinking, the driver is still drowsy despite an open-eye state.

5.5 FEATURE COMPUTATION

This section details the computation of the facial features utilized in the proposed system, namely EAR, MAR, blink count and duration, head position estimation, and eyeball movement. These features form the foundation for robust and real-time analysis of driver drowsiness, attentiveness, and fatigue levels.

5.5.1 EAR Computation

The Eye Aspect Ratio is commonly applied as a geometric indicator for analyzing eye state, including eye openness, closure, and blinking activity. It is calculated using Euclidean distance relationships among selected eye landmark points. In this work, these landmarks are not manually defined or obtained from fixed templates; instead, they are automatically estimated from each video frame through the SVM-based facial landmark prediction framework introduced in the previous chapter, which enables consistent and adaptive eye-state analysis under real-time operating conditions.

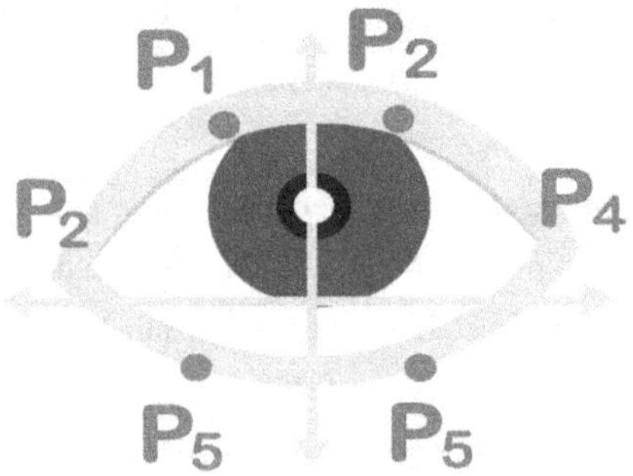

Figure 5.2. Visualization of the eye landmarks for EAR computation

Figure 5.2 shows the locations of six critical eye landmarks that are predicted directly from facial images using the trained SVM-based regression model. These points represent the horizontal eye corners along with the vertical eyelid landmarks positioned on the upper and lower eye contours. The adopted landmark estimation strategy is designed to handle moderate variations in head pose, since it learns spatial relationships among facial structures rather than assuming a perfectly frontal face alignment. This characteristic is essential in practical driving conditions, where small head rotations and tilts frequently occur. Using these predicted landmarks, the Eye Aspect Ratio is calculated through Euclidean distance measurements, as defined in Equation 5.1. The resulting EAR value provides a scale-invariant and pose-tolerant representation of eye openness, which makes it suitable for real-time detection of blinking behavior and prolonged eye closure events.

$$\text{EAR} = \frac{||P_2 - P_6|| + ||P_3 - P_5||}{2 \times ||P_1 - P_4||} \tag{5.1}$$

Here, P_1 and P_4 denote the horizontal eye landmark points located at the eye corners, whereas P_2 and P_6, together with P_3 and P_5, correspond to the vertical eye landmarks along the upper and lower eyelids. The term $|| P_a$ - $P_b||$ represents the Euclidean distance measured between any two landmark points P_a and P_b. Because the Eye Aspect Ratio remains relatively stable when the eyes are open and exhibits a rapid decrease during blinking or prolonged eye closure, it functions as a reliable indicator for continuous eye-state monitoring in real-time video streams.

5.5.2 MAR Computation

The computation of the Mouth Aspect Ratio (MAR) is based on the geometric relationships among eight mouth landmarks, which are automatically extracted from each facial image using the same SVM-based facial landmark prediction model described in Chapter 4. This landmark detection process operates directly on the input image and does not rely on manual annotation or strict frontal-face assumptions.

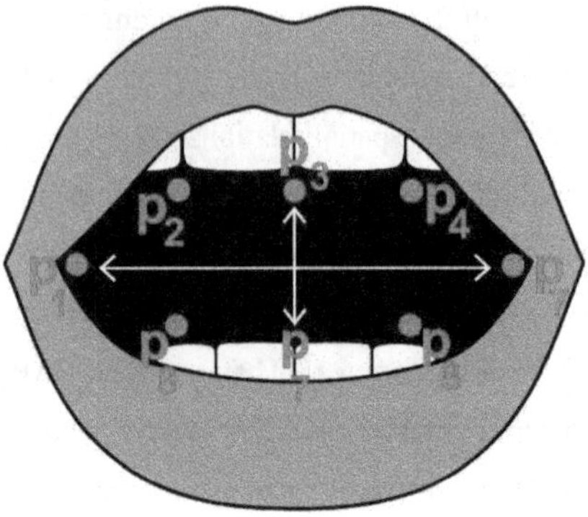

Figure 5.3. Visualization of the mouth landmarks for MAR computation

Figure 5.3 illustrates the eight key mouth landmarks used for MAR computation, including the horizontal mouth corner points and the vertical landmarks along the upper and lower lip contours. These landmarks are predicted by the trained regression model, which learns spatial facial relationships and is therefore resilient to moderate in-plane rotations and slight head pose variations commonly encountered in real driving conditions. As a result, accurate mouth landmark localization can still be achieved even when the face is not perfectly aligned with the camera. The MAR value is derived using the Euclidean distances between corresponding vertical lip landmarks and normalized by the horizontal mouth width. This normalization makes MAR scale-invariant and less sensitive to distance from the camera or individual differences in mouth size, thereby enabling robust detection of mouth opening events associated with yawning and early fatigue.

$$\text{MAR} = \frac{||P_2 - P_8|| + ||P_3 - P_7|| + ||P_4 - P_6||}{2 \times ||P_1 - P_5||} \tag{5.2}$$

In this formulation, P_1 and P_5 indicate the horizontal corner points of the mouth, whereas P_2 and P_8 correspond to the outer vertical landmarks of the upper and lower lips. Similarly, P_3 and P_7 denote the middle vertical lip landmarks, and P_4 and P_6 represent the inner vertical lip points. The notation $||\ P_a$ - $P_b||$ refers to the Euclidean distance measured between any two landmark points. During yawning, the vertical separation between the lips increases noticeably relative to the mouth width and remains elevated for a short duration; therefore, the Mouth Aspect Ratio serves as a dependable geometric measure for detecting yawning behavior and analyzing fatigue in real-time video streams.

5.5.3 Blink Rate

Blinks are detected by monitoring temporal fluctuations in the Eye Aspect Ratio (EAR) across consecutive video frames. In the proposed system, a blink event is precisely defined using two fixed EAR thresholds determined through empirical analysis conducted during system calibration and real-time experimentation. Specifically, a blink is identified when the EAR value falls below a lower threshold of 0.20 and subsequently rises above an upper threshold of 0.25, indicating a complete eye closure and reopening cycle. These threshold values ($T_{low} = 0.20$ and $T_{high} = 0.25$) were selected based on repeated real-time observations across multiple subjects, ensuring reliable separation between natural eye blinks, partial eye closure, and sustained eye closure associated with drowsiness. The use of two thresholds introduces hysteresis into the detection process, which helps prevent false blink detections caused by noise or minor EAR oscillations. The total blink count and the duration of each blink are computed within a sliding temporal window of 60 consecutive frames (approximately 2 seconds at 30 fps). This window length was chosen to balance temporal sensitivity and robustness, allowing the system to capture short-term blink dynamics without being overly sensitive to isolated frame-level variations.

Both blink frequency and blink duration serve as critical indicators of driver fatigue. An increased blink duration or a reduction in blink frequency, particularly when combined with other cues such as reduced EAR or head tilt, is strongly correlated with the onset and progression of drowsiness.

For each frame

Compute EAR for the current frame (EAR_t)

If $EAR_t < T_{low}$ and previous state is open

- Set state to "closed"
- Record blink start time/frame

If $EAR_t < T_{high}$ and previous state is closed

- Set state to "open"
- Record blink end time/frame
- Increment blink count
- Calculate blink duration

5.5.4 Head Pose Estimation

Head pose estimation refers to the process of determining the orientation of the driver's head, including forward-facing posture as well as slight or pronounced tilts in different directions. This estimation is obtained using three-dimensional facial landmark coordinates together with a projective geometric model to compute the yaw angle representing left–right rotation, the pitch angle representing upward or downward tilt, and the roll angle representing lateral inclination. Within the scope of this thesis, emphasis is placed on the pitch component, since downward head tilt was widely reported as a strong behavioral sign of fatigue and reduced alertness during driving activities. In this framework, excessive head movement is quantitatively characterized by evaluating both the magnitude and the temporal persistence of pitch angle deviation from the neutral upright position, as defined below.

- **Pitch angle between 0° and 10°** → Head is considered upright, indicating an alert driving state.
- **Pitch angle between 10° and 25° sustained for more than 1 second** → Classified as a slight downward tilt, associated with early fatigue or pre-drowsiness.
- **Pitch angle ≥ 25° sustained for more than 2 consecutive seconds** → Classified as a strong downward head tilt, indicating a high likelihood of deep drowsiness or microsleep episodes.

Head nodding is identified when repeated transitions between upright and strong downward pitch angles occur within a short temporal window (≤ 3 seconds), which is commonly observed during microsleep events. These quantified thresholds were empirically derived through repeated real-time observations across multiple test subjects, ensuring consistency with natural driving behavior while minimizing false positives caused by normal posture adjustments. The three-dimensional coordinate system used for head pose estimation, including the definition of yaw, pitch, and roll axes, is illustrated in Figure 5.4, which serves as the geometric reference for computing the driver's head orientation in real time.

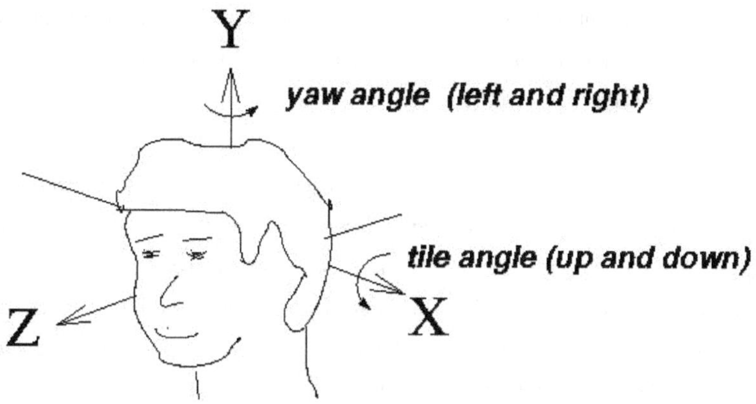

Figure 5.4. Illustration of head pose estimation

Figure 5.4 depicts the estimation of head pose within a three-dimensional coordinate framework, where the yaw angle represents left–right rotational movement about the Y-axis, and the pitch angle represents upward or downward rotation about the X-axis. Head pose estimation determines the spatial orientation of the driver's head by modeling three-dimensional rotations and translations, which are obtained through alignment of predefined 3D facial landmark reference points with their corresponding two-dimensional projections detected in the facial image. This geometric alignment process enables accurate representation of head orientation under natural driving movements.

Although human faces exhibit inter-individual anatomical variability, the proposed system employs a generic 3D head model for head pose estimation, which is a widely accepted and validated assumption in computer vision–based driver monitoring systems. This is justified because head pose estimation relies on relative geometric relationships between facial landmarks rather than absolute anatomical dimensions. The Perspective-n-Point (PnP) formulation estimates orientation by minimizing reprojection error between corresponding 3D–2D landmark pairs, making the solution invariant to moderate differences in facial size, ethnicity, and individual morphology, as long as the relative configuration of landmarks is preserved. Furthermore, the objective of head pose estimation in this work is not biometric identification, but coarse-to-moderate estimation of head orientation (upright, slightly tilted, strongly tilted), which is sufficient for detecting fatigue-related behaviors such as nodding and prolonged downward tilt. Therefore, a generic head model provides a robust and computationally efficient approximation, particularly suitable for real-time deployment on embedded platforms. Accordingly, the computation of head pose estimation is treated as a Perspective-n-Point (PnP) problem, as described below:

1. The algorithm selects a subset of stable and anatomically consistent facial landmarks, whose approximate 3D locations are known with respect to a generic head coordinate system (e.g., nose tip, chin, eye corners, and mouth corners). These landmarks are chosen because they exhibit minimal relative displacement across individuals and facial expressions, making them reliable reference points for pose estimation. The selected 3D model points are represented in Equation (5.3).

$$\text{Model Points (3D)} = \begin{bmatrix} X_1 & Y_1 & Z_i \\ X_2 & Y_2 & Z_2 \\ \vdots & \vdots & \vdots \\ X_n & Y_n & Z_n \end{bmatrix} \tag{5.3}$$

2. Second, a facial landmark detection model is applied to locate the corresponding two-dimensional image coordinates of the selected facial points, as expressed in Equation 5.4.

$$\text{Image Points (2D)} = \begin{bmatrix} x_1 & y_1 \\ x_2 & y_2 \\ \vdots & \vdots \\ x_n & y_n \end{bmatrix} \tag{5.4}$$

3. The algorithm estimates the intrinsic parameters of the camera, including focal length and optical center, and constructs the corresponding camera matrix KKK, as defined in Equation 5.5.

$$\text{Image Points (2D)} = \begin{bmatrix} f_x & 0 & c_x \\ 0 & f_y & c_y \\ 0 & 0 & 1 \end{bmatrix} \tag{5.5}$$

4. The algorithm utilizes an explicit algorithm to estimate the rotation vector r and translation vector t that best map the 3D model points to the 2D image points (Eivazi Adli, Shoaran and Sayyed Noorani, 2020). This process is mathematically given as follows in Equ 5.6:

$$(\mathrm{R}, \mathrm{t}) = \arg\min_{\mathrm{R,t}} \sum_{i=1}^{n} ||x_i - \pi(\mathrm{K}[\mathrm{R}|t]X_i||^2 \qquad (5.6)$$

From Equ 5.6, Where, X_i denotes 3D model points, x_i is the 2D image points, K camera intrinsic matrix, $\pi()$ indicates projection from 3D to 2D, R, t denotes rotation and translation to estimate, respectively.

5. Finally, the rotation vector rrr is converted into a rotation matrix, from which the yaw, pitch, and roll angles are extracted as Euler angles to represent the three-dimensional orientation of the head.

5.5.5 Eye Ball Movement computation

Eyeball movement is an important parameter in driver drowsiness monitoring as it helps in understanding pre-drowsy indicators like microsleeps, gaze shift, and a decrease in the focus. The tracking of eyeball movement lets the system know when a driver is losing attention, frequently closes his eyes, or is simply fatigued. The computation of eye ball movement starts with the detection of the iris, which involves computing the center position of the iris based on the eye region.

The following iris position across frames helps to measure horizontal movement and vertical movement. The eyeless research investigates the shift in gaze, prolonged fixation, and "saccadic" movement so that it is easier to detect fatigue/drowsiness. Another important factor considered when looking at eyeball movement is node. If the system detects repeated downward eye movements, the head could also be tilting downward, which is behaviour strongly associated with sleepiness. Ultimately this analysis is enhanced further as head pose estimation allows for both accounting for eyeball movement and head posture being used to make a fuller picture of drowsiness.

As illustrated in Figure 5.5, the iris refers to the circular, colored region of the human eye situated between the cornea and the lens, surrounding the pupil, which appears as the dark central opening. The primary function of the iris is to regulate the amount of light entering the eye by controlling pupil diameter through the contraction and relaxation of small muscular structures. These muscles adjust the pupil size by either expanding or constricting it in response to surrounding illumination levels. In adults, the iris typically has a diameter of approximately 11–12 mm, whereas the pupil exhibits dynamic variation depending on lighting conditions and cognitive or physiological state, usually ranging between 10% and 20% of the iris diameter under normal conditions. This natural variability enables effective regulation of light reaching the retina and is governed by the coordinated action of the iris sphincter and dilator muscles (Eliasdottir, 2018; Wyatt, 1995).

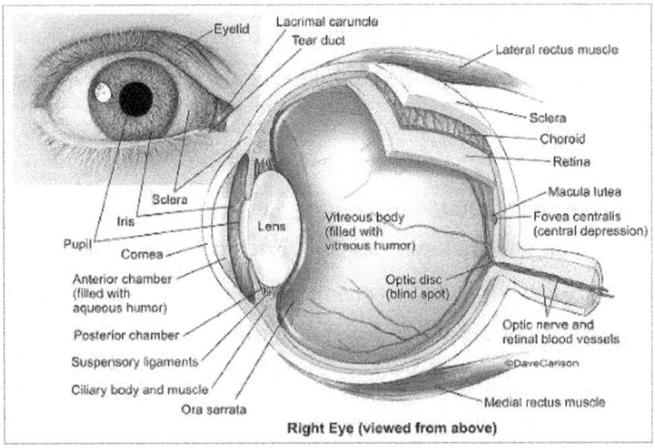

Figure 5.5. A Front and Side View of the Human Eye (Eliasdottir, 2018)

The iris is made up of several anatomical layers, each with distinct functional roles. The innermost layer, known as the pigmented epithelial layer, contains dense pigment cells that determine eye color and block excess light from entering the eye. Above this there is stroma, which consists of connective tissue, blood vessels, pigment cells, and two smooth muscles (the sphincter and dilator muscles) that regulate pupil size. The outer region of the iris exhibits two visually distinguishable zones: the inner pupillary zone surrounding the pupil and the outer ciliary zone, which are separated by a visible, irregular boundary known as the collarette (Eliasdottir, 2018; Wyatt, 1995). In the proposed detection system, Canny edge detection is first applied to extract prominent intensity gradients within the eye region, enabling reliable localization of iris and pupil boundaries (the Canny algorithm is formally described in Section 5.5.6).

The canny edge detection is selected due to its robustness to noise and its ability to preserve thin, continuous edges, which is critical for eye-region analysis (Canny, 1986). Once the system verifies that the eyes are open using EAR-based validation, the Circular Hough Transform (CHT) is applied to detect circular patterns corresponding to the iris boundary (the

CHT formulation and implementation are detailed in Section 5.5.7). The successful detection of circular contours across consecutive frames indicates active iris displacement, which reflects eye movement and sustained visual engagement, suggesting an alert driver state. In low-illumination or night-time conditions, especially for drivers with dark irises, the contrast between the pupil and iris may be significantly reduced, which can limit the reliability of direct iris boundary detection. To address this limitation, the proposed system does not rely solely on iris detection, but instead uses iris-based cues only when sufficient edge confidence is available, and complements them with EAR trends, blink duration, head pose, and fuzzy logic–based multi-feature fusion. If no reliable circular contours are detected and concurrent EAR and blink-duration indicators confirm eye closure, the system interprets this condition as drowsiness rather than a detection failure. In such cases, an alert is triggered according to the fuzzy inference outcome, ensuring robustness under varying lighting conditions.

5.5.6 Canny Edge Detection Algorithm

In the proposed framework, the Canny edge detection method is applied to precisely detect the boundary contours of both the pupil and the iris. Canny edge detection is commonly adopted in computer vision because it provides an effective balance between noise reduction, accurate edge localization, and continuity of detected edges, which makes it appropriate for detailed structural analysis tasks such as segmentation of the eye region (Canny, 1986; Zhu et al., 2022).

The first step of the algorithm involves noise reduction, which refers to unwanted intensity fluctuations introduced by sensor noise, illumination variations, or compression artifacts that may generate false edges in facial images. For example, random pixel-level brightness variations around the eye caused by low-light conditions or camera sensors can be misinterpreted as edges. To mitigate this, a Gaussian filter is applied to smooth the image, suppressing high-frequency noise while preserving meaningful edge structures. After smoothing, the algorithm computes intensity gradients, which represent spatial changes in pixel brightness. Edges correspond to locations where there is a sharp change in intensity, such as the transition between the iris and sclera or between the eyelid and surrounding skin. Identifying these changes allows the system to localize object boundaries accurately. The gradient magnitude is computed using the Euclidean norm, as shown in Eq. (5.7), because it provides a rotationally invariant and computationally efficient measure of edge strength, which is well suited for real-time eye-feature extraction.

$$|G| = \sqrt{G_X^2 + G_Y^2} \quad (5.7)$$

Where, G_x represents the image intensity gradient in the horizontal (x) direction, G_y represents the image intensity gradient in the vertical (y) direction, and $|G|$ denotes the gradient magnitude, which quantifies the strength of an edge at a given pixel. The gradient magnitude measures how rapidly the image intensity changes at a pixel location; larger values indicate stronger edges, such as the boundary between the iris and sclera or eyelid contours. This formulation is computationally efficient and rotationally invariant, making it suitable for real-time eye-feature extraction (Canny, 1986). After computing the gradient magnitude, the gradient direction is estimated to determine the orientation of the detected edge. This step is essential because edges in images are typically several pixels wide, and their exact location must be refined. The gradient direction is calculated as:

$$\theta = \arctan g \frac{Gx}{Gy} \quad (5.8)$$

Where, θ denotes the edge orientation angle, and G_x and G_y are the horizontal and vertical gradients, respectively. This equation basically estimates the direction of maximum intensity change, which is perpendicular to the edge. Knowing the edge direction allows the algorithm to correctly suppress non-edge pixels in subsequent steps, improving localization accuracy.

After computing the image gradients, Non-Maximum Suppression is applied to refine the detected edges. In this step, each pixel is evaluated by comparing its gradient magnitude with neighboring pixels along the corresponding gradient direction, and pixels that do not represent a local maximum are removed. This operation converts broad edge responses into thin, single-pixel-wide contours, which improves boundary localization accuracy (Canny, 1986; Zhu et al., 2022). Following this refinement, a double-threshold procedure is employed to categorize edge pixels into strong edges, weak edges, and non-edge regions based on two predefined threshold values, which supports reliable edge continuity and noise suppression.

- **Strong edges** exceed the high threshold and are immediately retained.

- **Weak edges** lie between the high and low thresholds and are retained only if they are connected to strong edges.
- **All other pixels are discarded.**

This hysteresis-based edge tracking ensures that true edges are preserved while noise-induced or isolated responses are removed, resulting in stable and meaningful boundary detection under varying illumination conditions (Canny, 1986).

5.5.7 Circular Hough Transform Algorithm

The Circular Hough Transform (CHT) (Duda and Hart, 1972) is a classical computer vision technique used for detecting circular shapes in images by exploiting the geometric definition of a circle. In the proposed system, the radius of the pupil and iris is not fixed but constrained within a physiologically plausible range, which makes the CHT suitable for robust eye-region analysis under real-time conditions. The method identifies circular structures by mapping edge points from the image space into a parameter space, where the most likely circle parameters (center and radius) are determined based on voting consistency. In this work, the CHT is applied exclusively for circular feature detection (pupil and iris), while line detection is not considered, and the detected circle parameters are used to estimate eyeball position and movement, as defined in Equ. (5.9).

$$R^2 = (x - a)^2 + (y - b)^2 \qquad (5.9)$$

Where, r is the radius, the center coordinates are represented by a and b. Using the parametric form, any point lying on the circumference of the circle can be described using the following expressions shown in Equ 5.10 and 5.11.

$$x = a + r\,cos(\theta) \qquad (5.10)$$

$$y = b + r\,sin(\theta) \qquad (5.11)$$

In order to detect the pupil or iris, the eye region is first localized from the facial image using the detected eye landmarks. Edge points within this region are extracted, and the Circular Hough Transform (CHT) (Duda and Hart, 1972) is applied to identify circular structures corresponding to the pupil or iris. For each detected edge point (x,y), a set of candidate circles with radii constrained to a physiologically valid range is generated, and each candidate votes in a Hough Space, which is a three-dimensional accumulator defined over the circle parameters (a,b,r), where (a,b) represents the center and r the radius. The Hough Space is constructed by incrementing accumulator values for all parameter combinations that satisfy the circle equation for a given edge point. After processing all edge points, peaks in the accumulator correspond to parameter sets that receive the highest number of votes, indicating strong circular evidence. The circle parameters associated with the maximum peak are selected as the detected pupil or iris, providing robust estimation of its center and radius, as illustrated in Figure 5.6.

Figure 5.6. Visualization of the eyeball movement

5.6 FUZZY LOGIC

Fuzzy logic represents a rule-based reasoning paradigm that was originally introduced to model human decision-making processes in situations characterized by uncertainty and imprecision, where system states cannot be described using strict binary boundaries (Zadeh, 1965). It provides a mathematical framework for reasoning and decision-making when available information is vague, incomplete, or uncertain. Unlike conventional binary logic, in which a condition is evaluated as either true or false, fuzzy logic allows variables to assume degrees of truth, enabling partial membership across multiple states at the same time. This characteristic is particularly relevant for driver drowsiness detection, since fatigue does not occur as a sudden binary event. A driver does not instantly shift from an alert condition to sleep; rather, alertness decreases progressively through intermediate stages such as fatigue and mild drowsiness. Fuzzy logic captures this gradual transition by modeling alertness as a continuum, ranging from fully awake to highly drowsy, which makes it well suited for representing and analyzing varying levels of driver vigilance. The overall structure of the fuzzy logic–based decision framework used in this study is illustrated in Figure 5.7.

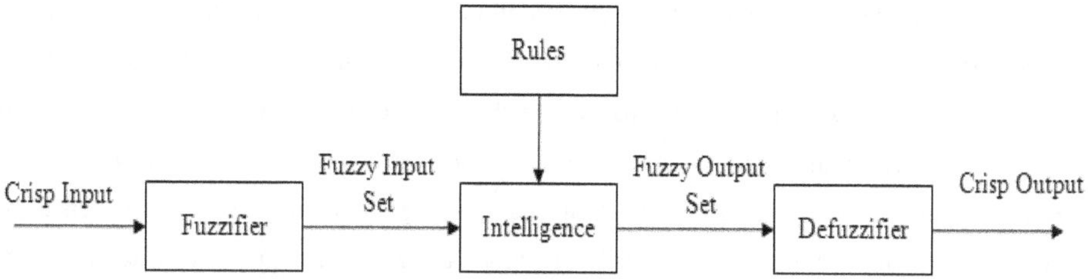

Figure 5.7. Illustrates the standard architecture of the fuzzy logic–based decision system adopted in this study

- **Fuzzifier (Fuzzification):** The fuzzification stage transforms the *crisp numerical inputs* produced by the vision-based modules, including Eye Aspect Ratio, Mouth Aspect Ratio, head position angle, eyeball movement, blink duration, and abrupt EAR variations, into corresponding *fuzzy input sets*. This transformation uses predefined membership functions that assign each input value to linguistic categories such as *Low, Medium,* and *High*. By performing this mapping, the system manages uncertainty and smooth behavioral transitions more effectively, instead of depending on fixed threshold boundaries.
- **Rule Base:** The *Rules* block represents the set of expert-defined IF–THEN rules that govern the decision-making process. These rules describe how combinations of fuzzy inputs correspond to different driver alertness states. In the proposed system, all fuzzy rules are explicitly defined and summarized in Table 5.7, which serves as the complete rule repository for the inference process.
- **Inference Engine (Intelligence block):** The inference engine evaluates the activated rules by computing the degree of match between the fuzzy input sets and the rule antecedents. Based on this matching, the engine combines the outputs of all relevant rules to produce a *fuzzy output set* that represents the inferred drowsiness level.
- **Defuzzifier (Defuzzification):** The Defuzzifier converts the aggregated fuzzy output set into a single *crisp output value*, referred to as the drowsiness score. This score is subsequently mapped to discrete driver states (Fully Active, Fatigue, Slightly Drowsy, Very Drowsy), enabling adaptive alert generation.

Step 1: Fuzzification (Defining Input Variables): Fuzzification refers to the transformation of crisp numerical values produced by the vision-based measurement modules into *fuzzy linguistic variables* through predefined membership functions. This step is necessary because physiological and behavioral indicators related to driver drowsiness do not follow strict or fixed boundaries; instead, their values change gradually across different drivers and driving situations. In this framework, each extracted feature, such as Eye Aspect Ratio, Mouth Aspect Ratio, or head position angle, is mapped to one or more fuzzy sets using continuous membership functions. These functions assign a *membership degree* within the range [0,1] which reflects how strongly a given input value belongs to linguistic labels such as *Low, Medium*, or *High*. Relying on crisp threshold values, for example defining a fixed limit such as EAR < 0.25, can lead to unstable decisions when feature values fluctuate near boundary regions. The fuzzification process addresses this limitation by allowing partial membership across multiple states, which supports smooth transitions between alertness levels and reduces unnecessary false alarms. This conversion is applied to every processed video frame after feature extraction and before fuzzy rule evaluation, and it represents the initial stage of the fuzzy inference pipeline illustrated in Figure 5.7. The proposed system applies fuzzification to six behavioral and physiological indicators closely associated with driver alertness, and these inputs along with their linguistic categories are summarized in Table 5.2.

Table 5.2. Highlights of Input variables used

Input Variables	Fuzzy Set (Categories)
EAR	Low, Medium, High
MAR	Low, Medium, High
Head Position	Upright, Slight Tilt, Full Tilt
Eye Ball Movement	Low, Medium, High
Blink Duration	Normal, Slightly Prolonged, Prolonged, Very Prolonged
Sudden EAR Increase	Yes, No

Step 2: Fuzzy Inference System (FIS): The FIS module applies IF-THEN fuzzy rules to determine the driver's drowsiness level based on various input conditions. Unlike rigid threshold-based systems, fuzzy logic accounts for uncertainty and gradual transitions between drowsiness levels. Here, each input variable (such as EAR, MAR, head position,

etc.) is assigned a membership function, which defines fuzzy categories corresponding to different states of drowsiness. These membership functions help to determine how strongly a given input belongs to a particular category, ensuring a smooth and adaptive classification of drowsiness levels. Table 5.3 shows fuzzy membership function defined in the proposed research.

Table 5.3. Fuzzy Membership Functions

Input Variable	Fuzzy Category	Range	Interpretation
EAR (Eye Openness)	Low	0.0 - 0.25	Eyes are nearly closed (high drowsiness risk).
	Medium	0.25 - 0.32	Eyes are slightly open (possible fatigue).
	High	0.32 - 0.50	Eyes are fully open (alert state).
MAR (Mouth Openness - Yawning)	Low	0.0 - 0.30	Mouth is closed (no yawning, alert state).
	Medium	0.30 - 0.50	Slightly open mouth (early fatigue signs).
	High	0.50 - 1.5	Yawning detected (drowsiness increasing).
Head Position (Tilt Angle)	Upright	0° - 10°	Normal posture (fully awake).
	Slight Tilt	10° - 25°	Early drowsiness signs.
	Full Tilt	≥ 25°	Likely nodding off (high drowsiness risk).
Eyeball Movement	Low	Normal horizontal movement	Alert state, normal behavior.
	Medium	Slowed movement, occasional downward motion	Early signs of drowsiness.
	High	Frequent downward movement, microsleeps	Strong indicator of drowsiness.

Blink Duration	Normal	< 1 second	Typical blink duration, no fatigue.
	Slightly Prolonged	1 - 2 seconds	Blink duration is increasing (early fatigue).
	Prolonged	2 - 3 seconds	High risk of drowsiness.
	Very Prolonged	> 3 seconds	Critical drowsiness, immediate danger.
Sudden EAR Increase	Yes	Detects forced wakefulness	Indicates the driver is struggling to stay awake.
	No	No forced wakefulness detected	Natural state, normal driver behavior.

The numerical ranges defined in Table 5.3 were established through a combination of values commonly reported in the driver drowsiness literature and empirical observations obtained during real-time experimental testing of the proposed system. For EAR, values below 0.25 consistently corresponded to eye closure or near-closure, while values above 0.32 reflected alert eye openness; the intermediate range was introduced to model transitional fatigue states. Similarly, MAR thresholds were selected to distinguish closed-mouth conditions (<0.30), partial opening associated with early fatigue (0.30–0.50), and yawning behavior (>0.50). Head tilt angle ranges were defined based on observed posture changes, where angles below 10° indicated an upright head position and angles exceeding 25° were associated with sustained downward tilt or nodding. Blink duration thresholds were derived from temporal eye-closure analysis, with durations exceeding two seconds indicating severe drowsiness or microsleep risk. Eyeball movement patterns and sudden EAR increases were modeled qualitatively to capture microsleep-related gaze shifts and forced wakefulness attempts. The use of overlapping fuzzy ranges allows the system to accommodate inter-individual variability and gradual transitions between alertness states, avoiding rigid thresholding while ensuring stable real-time performance.

The fuzzy rule set integrates six complementary features such as EAR, MAR, head position, eyeball movement, blink duration, and sudden EAR increase rather than relying solely on EAR and MAR. This multi-feature integration allows the system to model drowsiness as a progressive and contextual phenomenon, thereby improving robustness and reducing false alarms in real-world driving scenarios. The rules were formulated based on empirical observations and established behavioral patterns reported in the literature. Table 5.4 summarizes the adaptive fuzzy rule base, where the drowsiness level is the primary decision outcome and each level is associated with an appropriate alert action.

Step 3: Fuzzy Rule Set: The fuzzy rule set integrates six complementary features such as EAR, MAR, head position, eyeball movement, blink duration, and sudden EAR increase rather than relying solely on EAR and MAR. This multi-feature integration allows the system to model drowsiness as a progressive and contextual phenomenon, thereby improving robustness and reducing false alarms in real-world driving scenarios. The rules were formulated based on empirical observations and established behavioral patterns reported in the literature. Table 5.4 summarizes the adaptive fuzzy rule base, where the drowsiness level is the primary decision outcome and each level is associated with an appropriate alert action.

Table 5.4. Adaptive fuzzy rule base for drowsiness detection

EAR	MAR	Head Position	Eye Ball Movement	Blink Duration	Sudden EAR Increase	Drowsiness Level	Alert Type
High	Low	Upright	Low	Normal	No	Fully Active	No alert
Medium	Medium	Slightly Tilted	Medium	Slightly Prolonged	No	Fatigue	Alert for rest
Medium	High	Upright	Low	Slightly Prolonged	No	Fatigue	Alert for rest
Low	Medium	Downward Tilt	High	Prolonged (1–2 s)	No	Slightly Drowsy	Mild alert
Very Low	Low	Strong Downward Tilt	High	Prolonged (1–2 s)	No	Slightly Drowsy	Mild alert
Very Low	High	Downward Tilt	High	Prolonged (1–2 s)	No	Very Drowsy	High-risk alert
Very Low	High	Strong Downward Tilt	High	Very Prolonged (>2 s)	No	Very Drowsy	Emergency alert

		Tilt		(>2 s)			
High (Sudden Increase)	Medium	Slightly Tilted	High	Slightly Prolonged	Yes	Slightly Drowsy (Struggling to Stay Awake)	Mild alert
High (Sudden Increase)	High	Downward Tilt	High	Prolonged	Yes	Very Drowsy (Struggling to Stay Awake)	Emergency alert

Step 4: Defuzzification (Generating a Crisp Output): The defuzzification process converts fuzzy drowsiness levels into a numerical drowsiness score (0 - 100) and based on this different alert is generated as mentioned in Table 5.5.

Table 5.5. Adaptive rule base

Drowsiness Score	Classification	Alert Type
0 - 30	Fully Awake	No Alert
31 - 50	Fatigue	Alert for rest
51 - 65	Slightly Drowsy	Mild alert
66 - 100	Very Drowsy	Emergency alert

Table 5.5 illustrates the adaptive mapping between the system's fuzzy drowsiness score and the corresponding driver state classification and alert mechanism. The drowsiness score is a continuous output generated by the fuzzy inference system, reflecting the real-time integration of all monitored behavioral and physiological indicators. Rather than issuing binary or rigid alerts, the system supports graduated levels of response based on the driver's assessed risk:

5.7 RESULT AND ANALYSIS

The system was designed and implemented using the Python programming language, with model execution carried out through the Anaconda distribution on a Windows 10 platform.

This section presents an evaluation of the proposed driver drowsiness detection framework by analyzing its operational effectiveness and performance under the defined experimental setup. Unlike the previous chapters, where both publicly available and custom datasets were employed for training and evaluation, this chapter focuses on validating a novel fuzzy logic–based decision framework proposed by this research. Since the fuzzy rule base, membership functions, and multi-feature integration strategy are original contributions, no directly comparable state-of-the-art benchmark or labeled dataset exists in the literature for fair quantitative evaluation. Moreover, publicly available datasets primarily provide static labels and do not capture continuous behavioral transitions such as microsleeps, forced eye opening, or gradual fatigue progression, which are central to the proposed framework. Therefore, the system was evaluated using custom real-time video streams, allowing assessment of its adaptive, context-aware behavior under realistic operating conditions. This evaluation strategy is aligned with the real-time nature of the proposed system, while dataset-based benchmarking is identified as a direction for future work.

a) Very Drowsy **b) Fully Active**

Figure 5.8. Illustrates classification results, very drowsy and fully active states

The classification performance of the proposed algorithm for two different driver states, such as Very Drowsy and Fully Active based on real-time detection is illustrated in Figure 5.8. In the Very Drowsy state (Figure 5.8a), the system identifies severe drowsiness through a combination of very low EAR (eyes nearly closed), very high MAR (yawning), prolonged blink duration, and pronounced downward head tilt. As a result, the system generates a high-risk emergency alert. In contrast, in the Fully Active state (Figure 5.8b), the driver exhibits high EAR, low MAR, upright head posture, and normal blink duration, leading to no alert, thereby minimizing unnecessary driver distraction.

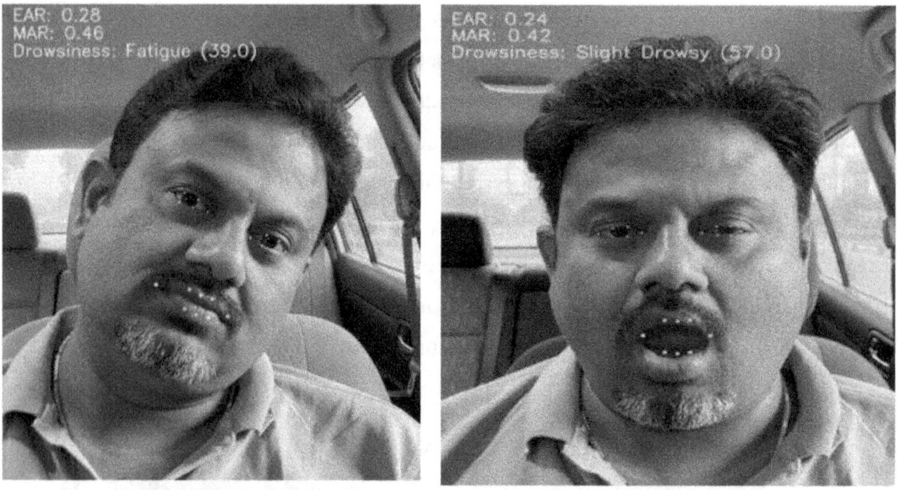

a) Fatigue **b) Slight Drowsy**

Figure 5.9. Classification results fatigue and slightly drowsy states

Figure 5.9 demonstrates the system's ability to distinguish intermediate alertness levels, namely Fatigue and Slightly Drowsy. In the Fatigue state (Figure 5.9a), the driver shows moderate head tilt, medium EAR, moderately increased MAR, and slightly prolonged blinks, triggering a rest warning alert. In the Slightly Drowsy state (Figure 5.9b), further reduction in EAR relative to the Fatigue state, increased MAR due to yawning, and blink durations between 1–2 seconds are observed, resulting in a mild drowsiness alert. Table 5.6 summarizes the obtained quantitative values recorded for all four driver states.

Table 5.6. Representative feature values for different driver states

Driver State	EAR	MAR	Blink Duration (s)	Head Tilt	Drowsiness Score	Alert Type
Fully Active	High	Low	< 1	Upright	Low	No Alert

Fatigue	Medium	Medium	~1	Slight	Moderate	Rest Alert
Slightly Drowsy	Low–Medium	High	1–2	Downward	High	Mild Alert
Very Drowsy	Very Low	Very High	> 2	Strong	Very High	Emergency Alert

The proposed fuzzy logic–based system was evaluated through real-time testing using live video streams, as its adaptive rule base and multi-feature integration are specifically designed for continuous, context-aware decision-making rather than static dataset classification. Since not directly comparable fuzzy-rule-driven real-time framework exists in the current literature, the evaluation focused on internal validation, demonstrating reliable differentiation between multiple drowsiness levels and timely alert generation. This provides a strong foundation for future benchmarking on standardized public datasets.

5.8 SUMMARY

This chapter introduced a real-time and adaptive driver drowsiness detection framework based on multi-feature fusion and fuzzy logic inference. The proposed system combines several behavioral and physiological indicators, including Eye Aspect Ratio, Mouth Aspect Ratio, head pose, blink duration, and eyeball movement, to represent driver alertness in an integrated and comprehensive manner. Experimental validation using real-time video streams showed that the framework reliably differentiates among multiple vigilance levels, namely Fully Active, Fatigue, Slightly Drowsy, and Very Drowsy, while generating appropriate alerts with minimal false alarms. Conventional deep learning models that rely on Softmax-based classification generally impose rigid class boundaries and do not explicitly represent uncertainty or gradual transitions between alertness states. In contrast, the fuzzy logic–driven decision mechanism supports human-like reasoning under uncertainty by allowing partial membership across multiple vigilance levels, which enables smooth state transitions rather than abrupt class changes. In addition, fuzzy logic offers transparent multi-feature integration and interpretable decision rules, which are important for real-time adaptive alerting and user trust in safety-critical automotive systems. The developed framework maintains low computational overhead and is suitable for deployment on embedded and real-world automotive platforms. Nevertheless, the use of manually defined membership functions and rule bases introduces dependency on prior design choices, which may require adjustment for drivers with different anatomical, behavioral, or cultural characteristics. Future extensions of this work may incorporate adaptive techniques such as Adaptive Neuro-Fuzzy Inference Systems or data-driven fuzzy rule learning to support automatic parameter tuning, enhanced personalization, and improved robustness across diverse driver populations.

CHAPTER-6

CONCLUSION

This research introduces a comprehensive and multi-layered solution for driver drowsiness detection that addresses critical challenges related to detection accuracy, generalization capability, real-time adaptability, and computational efficiency. The central aim of the thesis was to design a vision-based and context-aware framework for estimating driver Levels of Vigilance using advanced deep learning techniques combined with adaptive artificial intelligence methods, with a clear focus on practical real-time deployment scenarios.

The proposed framework was developed and validated through three core implementation phases, each evaluated in terms of accuracy, robustness, and real-time performance under diverse driving conditions. In the first phase, visual feature extraction was performed using CNN-based models, where EfficientNetV2B0 and ensemble learning approaches demonstrated strong performance, achieving classification accuracies of up to 98% and 99%, respectively. These results confirmed the effectiveness of deep convolutional architectures in capturing discriminative facial features related to driver fatigue. The second phase introduced a hybrid deep learning and machine learning framework, combining CNN probability outputs with SVM-based facial landmark analysis and a multi-stage decision fusion strategy. Real-time experiments using live webcam video streams validated the robustness of this approach in detecting critical drowsiness indicators such as prolonged eye closure and yawning, particularly under varying illumination and driver-specific conditions.

In the third phase, a lightweight fuzzy logic–based adaptive decision-making system was developed to classify driver alertness into multiple fatigue levels and generate context-sensitive alerts. By modeling drowsiness as a continuum rather than a binary state, the fuzzy inference system enabled more human-like and interpretable decision-making, while significantly reducing unnecessary or false alerts. This phase represents a key contribution of the thesis, as it bridges the gap between high-accuracy visual detection and practical, user-acceptable real-time alerting. In addition to the core framework, an exploratory investigation into hybrid quantum–classical neural networks (HQCNNs) were conducted and is presented separately in the appendix. This exploration study examined the feasibility of integrating quantum-inspired feature learning into driver monitoring tasks and achieved promising preliminary results under simulated conditions. However, this component is positioned as a forward-looking feasibility study rather than a primary contribution, and it is not intended to replace the classical systems developed in the main body of the thesis.

The findings of this research demonstrate that driver drowsiness detection can be significantly improved by integrating deep visual feature learning with adaptive, context-aware decision mechanisms. The proposed framework successfully combines high-performing CNN models with hybrid decision fusion and fuzzy logic–based reasoning, enabling robust real-time detection across multiple drowsiness levels while minimizing false alerts. Experimental evaluations confirm that modeling drowsiness as a gradual and context-dependent phenomenon, rather than a binary state, leads to more reliable and user-acceptable system behavior in practical driving scenarios. The core findings and significance of the proposed study is discussed as follows:

- **High classification performance:** EfficientNetV2B0 achieved up to 98% accuracy, while ensemble models reached 99% accuracy on visual drowsiness classification tasks.
- **Robust real-time detection:** Live webcam-based testing demonstrated reliable detection of critical cues such as prolonged eye closure, yawning, and head tilt under varying illumination and driver conditions.
- **Improved decision reliability:** The fuzzy logic–based alerting system reduced unnecessary alerts by adaptively classifying driver state into multiple vigilance levels rather than using rigid thresholds.
- **Enhanced interpretability:** The use of linguistic rules and physiological cues (EAR, MAR, blink duration, head pose) enabled transparent and human-interpretable decision-making.
- **Exploratory innovation:** The appendix-based HQCNN study demonstrated feasibility of quantum-inspired feature learning, achieving competitive performance under simulation and indicating potential for future extensions.

The research proposed in this thesis presents an effective computational framework for driver drowsiness detection which is a multi-level module and is highly synchronized and can be integrated into the deployment scenario of real tasks based on the contextual requirement. However, the scope of the proposed research work is not limited to its current implementation, in the future it can be extended towards on-device usability and a more optimized approach for edge computing platforms.

In future work, the proposed system can be extended towards incorporating multimodal signal physiological data such as heart rate, PPG, or skin conductivity along with visual cues for early detection of drowsiness and cognitive fatigue. The proposed research work can also be extended towards personalized driver modeling and recommendation systems. The currently proposed framework is developed on static thresholds, which may be affected due to inter-individual variability in fatigue responses and require adjustments in thresholds for a person with different racial backgrounds. In the future, more adaptive models such as ANFIS can be used that learn individual baselines over time, increasing the accuracy of the system and reducing false positives, making alerts more acceptable and effective. Furthermore, the deployment of intelligent driver drowsiness systems on embedded hardware is also an important area of interest where vehicles are equipped with increasingly powerful onboard processors, requiring adaptive deep learning models through compression, pruning, and quantum-inspired approximations. In addition, future work can also explore the application of intelligent human-machine interfaces that can enhance driver engagement. For example, multilingual AI voice assistants can issue customized natural-language alerts according to the driver's language and communication preferences, thereby improving both user compliance and system acceptance. To increase situational relevance, context-aware decision systems should incorporate environmental factors such as weather, time of day, or traffic density into the alerting logic, possibly using extended fuzzy rule sets or reinforcement learning. Finally, there is also scope for exploring federated learning for collaborative model training across multiple vehicles or users, allowing personalization without compromising driver privacy. Based on the above discussion, the directions for future research work can be highlighted as follows:

- Multimodal Signal Integration and Personalized Driver Modeling
- Use of Adaptive Neuro-Fuzzy Inference Systems (ANFIS)
- On-Device Deployment and Optimization
- AI-Powered Multilingual Voice Assistants
- Context-Aware Decision
- Making and Federated Learning for Privacy-Preserving Personalization

www.ingramcontent.com/pod-product-compliance
Lightning Source LLC
LaVergne TN
LVHW010728061126
851857LV00014B/1391
* 9 7 9 8 2 4 0 8 8 6 3 6 2 *